DEDICATION

I dedicate this book to the pilot training classmates from 48-B, living and dead, who also gained their experience in those aircraft following WWII.

ACKNOWLEDGMENTS

I owe a debt to those who I flew with during my lifetime, for providing me experience and the comradeship of those who fly. It was exciting mixing those long hours of boredom with those brief moments of terror. My heel marks still show on the ramp at my last air base....

INTRODUCTION

During the past years, I have set down stories about a specific flight or reminiscing about a certain airplane type. Assembling these stories results in an assembly of largely unrelated stories with little in the way of a common thread. The thread is that each story revealed some humor, danger, or the rigors of flying. During my flying career beginning with the solo in 1946 and ending with my last flight in 2012, I flew 65 different models of aircraft and 16,000 hours.

Like a lot of boys in the 30s and 40s I was interested in airplanes and flying more than any other activity. Toy airplanes, making model airplanes, reading about the pilots of old were my main trends of thought. The urge to get into flying became a goal by the early forties with WWII in progress. I proceeded to finish high school in 3 years [lacking a class in Geography and the fourth year of PT].

Seeking an Aviation Cadet slot, I signed up for the Air Corps Reserve in 1943 as soon as I was 17. The Air Corps entered me into a college program promoted by the AAF as soon as my third year of high school ended in June 1944. The reserve program went by the name Army Specialized Training Reserve Program (ASTRP). I went to the Michigan College of Mining and Technology in Houghton, MI for three-quarters. We were called to active duty and Basic Training in early 1945 that included the physical and Stanine testing for the Aviation Cadet selection. I was one of those selected as a Pilot trainee and sent to Smyrna, Tenn. for On-Line Training awaiting a Pre-flight assignment.

The war in Europe ended in May 1945 and greatly reduced the need for pilot training, and many of us went to air bases as On-line Trainees as a way to hold us for training if needed. When the Japanese surrendered in September 1945, the OLT people were assigned to technical schools. Again this was a holding point for activity while the wholesale discharge of WWII soldiers was worked out. I attended a Sheet Metal Specialist school at Chanute Field, IL. Others were scattered out to other schools. In my case, I 'graduated' from the Tech School on 1 Nov 1945 and was discharged the same day.

I re-entered the Air Corps in July 1946 as part of a light-hearted agreement with a school friend to go into the Army together for 18 months and get out and go to college. I was agreeable to getting back in the Army for that period, why I don't know because I already had enough service for the GI Bill. My friend, Duane Hooker, and I were separated at the induction center because my previous Air Corp service combined with the 18-month enlistment meant I had to go back to the Air Corps. I was disappointed for a short time, but got over it and started thinking of it as another adventure. They assigned me to Mather Field, CA and almost immediately that base sent me to Florida to attend a technical school to become a Radar Mechanic.

I applied for the Aviation Cadet training program, while still in the technical school, as soon as it was announced. I completed the tech school in the spring of 1947 and worked on the flight line as a beginner technician until my selection to pilot training came through. I and one additional applicant left for pilot training at Randolph Field, Texas in late June or early July 1947. Mather Field provided Ben Walker and me a ride in a B-25 to Randolph, so we felt pretty special since enlisted men in those days usually got a train ticket.

At Randolph, Ben and I joined the group of 802 students (600 Aviation Cadets, 207 Student Officers) to become Pilot Class 48-B. The class graduated a year later, graduating 323 new pilots (239 Cadets, and 84 Student Officers). The 60 percent washout rate was brutal, but from what I have read, it was expected by the Air Corps brass. Pilot Class 48-B had some distinctions in their training. We were the last class to fly the Stearman bi-plane of WWII fame, one-half of the class flew the former Advanced Trainer AT-6 in Primary, a first introduction to flight. We flew former combat aircraft for Advanced Training. Those in Single Engine Training flew the P-51. Those of us in multi-engine training flew the B-25. Some of the single engine trainees flew the new P-80. Despite training in complex aircraft early in the training cycle, only three student fatalities occurred during two accidents.

Assignments after training scattered the new pilots to bases all over the US. The US Army Air Corps had become the United States Air Force while we were in training. My first assignment, along with another new second lieutenant and a Captain, a former student officer, was with Air Rescue Service at March Field, CA. These units were situated all over the world and by in large were kept busy with their primary job. My first nine years as an Air Force pilot were with Air Rescue Service, and many of my memories are in those early assignments building experience.

Someone said that flying consists hours upon hours of boredom, broken up by a brief periods of sheer terror. At other times flying becomes a humorous event, funny or black humor. I selected these stories from some of these times, generally in the order they occurred.

During these years I flew many different types, from slow single engine 'light' planes to four engine aircraft. These included: Aeronca Champ, Stearman biplane, Ryan PT-22, AT-6, B-25, L-5, L-4, L-13, L-19, SA-10[PBY], SB-17, C-47, C-82, SA-16, T-33, RB-57A, RB-66, EC-121, T-39, F-100D and F, with the final active duty in the EB-57. I volunteered for a combat tour in the F-100, volunteered again for a tour as a Misty FAC during an assignment to Phu Cat, So South Vietnam.

After retirement, I flew about 6000 hours in light planes as an instructor pilot, Civil Air Patrol pilot, and as a charter pilot. Civilian airplanes I flew include the various models of the Piper Cub, and other Piper single engine planes, and Piper Twins. Cessna made airplanes included the 152, 172, 182, 210, 310, 340, 402, and Caravan. Beech made planes included the Musketeer, Bonanza and two versions of the Baron. I was an instructor in most of these and check airman in those used in the charter business.

THE NIGHT I FLEW WITH MAJOR MORK, or "I'll scrape the hull on that shack"

In 1948, I was assigned to Flight B of the 4th Air Rescue Squadron, a new Second Lieutenant out of flight school. The unit had several airplanes and two helicopters to use in the search and rescue business. This unit was located at March Field, California. As a fresh and inexperienced 2nd Lt, I spent most of my flying hours in the single engine over-powered light plane called the L-5. A nice light plane, 190 horsepower, light steel frame covered with fabric and plywood. It was a wonderful search plane, slow maneuverable and the big engine could get you out of trouble – yes and in trouble too, of course. The checkout was simple: Get in, the instructor tells you how to start it and he tells you something like: "Use 60 on final - See you." That was expected. We were rated pilots and had flown similar airplanes - uh aircraft, we were in the new Air Force – we didn't fly airplanes.

Most of my local and search hours were in the L-5, and loving it. The L-5 had two seats, but nearly all the time we flew alone –just the way we liked it. We had two L-5's in the squadron and two 2nd Lieutenants. That couldn't be a coincidence. The other 2nd Lt. was named Johnson, and neither was that a coincidence. Our duty station assignments out of flight school were alphabetical. We enjoyed those canvas fighters and soon were able to make a 300 ft. vertical climb immediately after takeoff by holding the plane on the ground or skimming the surface until we reached the end of this short taxiway we used as a runway. Exciting, and learning to fly at the same time, since we nosed over to level off at extremely slow speed and it was a no-no to lose altitude during the level off. We both got pretty good at it, and landings could be made hair-raising too. Supervision of this flying was pretty elementary. Don't break the aircraft and we will leave you alone.

In addition to the two L-5's, the unit had two SA-10[PBY], one SB-17, one C-47 for cargo, and two H-5 helicopters when I arrived at Flight B.

As time went on, the other 2nd Lt and I were checked out in the other ships in the squadron. Johnson was 'chosen' to fly the SB-17 and I was 'chosen' to fly the SA-10 [the Navy called it a PBY5A. We called the plane the PBY or P-Boat or Pig Boat,

and seldom referred to it as the SA-10. The PBY was an amphibian, a seaplane with wheels and although we were quite a ways from the water, our area of responsibility had plenty. The unit was expected to execute a sea rescue if needed, so those that flew the plane got some water training. I think we both were getting time in the C-47 Goony Bird.

Johnson and I were launched very often on search missions since both of us wanted to fly more than the other, so the scheduler had an easy choice when a mission came up. Most of our flights were in the L-5's, but we were available to fly anytime anywhere in anything. Those were exciting times too, flying contour searches in the mountains, mixed in with the boring back and forth land search. Many missions were false or premature, but they were all interesting.

One of the unusual and memorable missions was a search mission flown out of Santa Barbara in the mountains north of the city and well west of Los Angeles. The airport was perfect as a search base, as it had all the services necessary, was close to the search mission and a particular hotel specialized in steamship round beef dinners. After flying two four-hour search missions with only a sandwich and water, that steamship round was the answer to our dreams. The object of this search was a small low wing plane flying from the San Francisco area to the Los Angeles area but failed to show up at the destination. Typical of those days, no flight plan, no weather briefing, no idea of the proposed flight path. We scoured the countryside. Suddenly it was announced that the FBI was interested in this search and the airplane. They wouldn't tell us then, but the pilot was carrying some classified papers in the plane to take to a meeting.

Finally, one afternoon the plane was spotted by one of the search planes and a ground team was immediately organized. The FBI decided to send two agents to go with the ground rescue team. What little could be observed from the search aircraft, the canopy was missing, and the cockpit of the low wing plane seemed to be empty. As the ground team was being organized and equipment assembled, it was apparent they would be in the mountains all night and they didn't have enough food and other equipment. So the co-pilot on the PBY was corralled and went into town with the mission commander to pick up various supplies. The operations officer tagged me to fly in the right seat of the PBY to fly co-pilot for Major John Mork. He was a very experienced pilot, especially flying the PBY/SA-10, having served in the Pacific during WWII flying this same type. In fact, he held a Distinguished Flying Cross for rescuing a pilot near a Japanese-held

island and accomplished the pickup of the pilot under heavy machine gun fire. He had a delicate touch for an aircraft of such heavy controls and a machine that had a mind of its own. One of the PBY's peculiar characteristics was a movement of the nose through a flat horizontal eight. This "Dutch Roll" was disconcerting and correcting it developed large leg muscles as you worked the rudder. When Major Mork flew the aircraft it did pretty much what he wanted.

The ground team departed with the two FBI agents and equipment they had as soon as they were organized. They had very little food since they couldn't wait for the trip into town to return with the goods. Buying the food and some hardware items were done through a Special form [Form 15] that was common at the time for making emergency purchases. The time-consuming part was explaining the procedure to the stores that had never used the form to receive payment. The plan was that the food and other supplies would be delivered to the fire tower using the aircraft. In the meantime, I spent the time with Major Mork planning our part of the supply drop, gathering together the cargo parachutes and looking at the maps of the area.

The crash was located near an abandoned fire watch tower like a lot of other towers that were located all over the forest. The tower was on the highest point of a ridgeline. The team indicated that would be the overnight campsite.

We made plans to tie safety lines to the crew connected to anchor points in the aircraft so they wouldn't fall out. They would be standing up and not be wearing safety belts. As I remember, they wore parachute harnesses and the safety lines connected to them. They didn't wear parachutes since they wouldn't be flying high enough to used them.

The ground rescue team reached the crash site near sundown,

and part of them moved on to the ranger tower to secure a campsite. We had received the goods from the downtown stores, gathered together the cargo parachutes needed and had them loaded on the PBY. Major Mork indicated we needed to get into the air and arrive at the ranger tower in time before dark. Major Mork briefed the procedure for the cargo drops out of the left side blister. The blister was a large Plexiglas enclosure that served as a search lookout location and during the war served as a machine gun position. We were to use the intercom to keep the crew in back informed of where we were and how far away from the drop. The final few seconds would be 'Countdown 3, 2, 1, DROP.' The cargo chute would open very close to the aircraft and immediately slow the package. It was not intended to float down, but slow as it was decelerating. The cargo would come to a stop, so the call to drop was made close to the target and anticipated slightly the delay in the crew throwing the chute and cargo clear of the blister.

The sun was disappearing below the Pacific shortly after takeoff and we took up the direct heading to the ranger tower. Finding it in the dusk was the easy part and the first low pass over it was to take a look at the approach and the terrain and obstacles around and near the site. The ground team or most of them were on site and ready to receive their supper and other goods. As the minutes passed the light was fading. The sun had gone below the horizon and it was getting dark. On the second pass, we could still see the tower when we turned towards it from the base leg or starting point. Major Mork set up the final approach somewhat parallel to the ridgeline to help guide us in and there were flashlights in the upper part of the tower – 'so the place wasn't locked after all' - Nice target. The crew in the back were ready to toss the package and the attached parachute out on my call. The chute was opened by static line but still the arrangement called for throwing them in the slipstream separately.

The first drop went off well. I called the drop hoping the chute would open and 'slow' the package. Damn that tower looked pretty close, much closer than I expected! Just as we passed the tower I had that feeling you get just before touchdown on the runway! The rescue team called out 'good drop!' and we made a climbing turn back to the start of the next run. Hey, this was fun! Major Mork told us that he was going to have to stay low so we could drop on the side facing us, as he noted earlier that the ridge fell off sharply just beyond the tower. We certainly didn't want to have the package land long. The second drop went well, but it was getting darker. The flashlights were still there, and a good thing, although as we got near the release point we could see they were all on the ground level. Maybe Mork got too low the first time. This drop went off well from our viewpoint [the cargo didn't hit the tower] but the parachute went just beyond the ridgeline and landed a short ways below.

By the third drop, it was well past what you would call dusk, but not what people call pitch black – you get the idea – it was dark. By this time, we had turned down the cockpit lights and used only the ultra-violet lamps that lit up only the numbers on the dials. These old birds still had a lot of instruments with radium and they stayed lit fairly well without the ultra-violet lights. This was the third and last package and Major Mork lined up well below the tower so he could make out the trees in the landing lights and be climbing during the drop instead of being in a descent. A couple hundred yards or so from the tower he called for climb power. He pushed up the throttles hanging from the ceiling and I quickly adjusted the RPM. We reached the drop point, and I counted down and called the drop. Very quickly, one of the crewmembers in the back called on the intercom "The package and chute are hung up on the gun mount." They indicated the drag from the slipstream was so much they couldn't pull them back into the blister area. Major Mork picked up his mike and said, "Get ready to cut those things loose, I'm going to scrape the hull on that shack!"

By this time, I am thinking that I am going to die that night in the PBY. Major. Mork turned to the opposite heading or downwind leg to get back to the point the start the run. Of course by now, it was darker. He brought the plane back around from the base leg to the start of the run and descended back down to the run-in altitude as he pointed the plane at the flashlights again – although now there are fewer flashlights. The crew in back got their knife [s] ready to cut the one line that was caught on the gun mount. It was dark, not a true pitch black, but semi-pitch black. You get the idea. It was dark-dark. We couldn't see much in the landing lights, but the few flashlights were dead ahead. It was exciting, but I managed to keep the tone of my voice down as I started the countdown to the drop. 'Jesus, that tower looks above us for sure.' Finally, the **3 2 1 DROP** call went out and the roof of the tower reached life size. At the time, and I haven't changed the notion, that the roof of the tower passed above the bottom of the hull and well inside the wingtip on Mork's side. Immediately after passing the tower and the objects lit by the landing lights, it was like staring into an ink bottle. Major Mork did a good job of instrument flying to get us up and around to take a final look at the lights on the ground before heading back to Santa Barbara and that beautiful steamship round. There was not much said on the intercom on the way back. Everybody was well aware of how close we came to that tower.

It wasn't a big thing to Major Mork. It was what he did and he 'had to do it' kind of thing. In my memory, the best PBY pilot I ever saw and no bragging on his part either. An example of this prowess, during a slow day they stood wheel chocks on the runway edge every couple hundred feet. Major. Mork made a touch and go landing and knocked over every other wheel chock. Basically, he was slow flying the plane with the wheel on the ground part of the time. No one else came close.

Now, I have my opinion of how close we came to the roof of the tower, and that was closer than I ever wanted to come. But when the ground team came back from the mission they had a different story. Before that, we need to know that the pilot was dead in the cockpit and the papers were all found, but scattered around the crash site. The team leader explained that after the first pass, no one wanted to be in the upper part of the tower – the living area – and they all went back down the steps to the ground. Long after the last pass while they were sitting around enjoying the meal we delivered so cleverly, the two FBI agents got into a heated argument. They were discussing how close the plane came to the tower. They were both firm in their convictions, and wouldn't change their mind. One said we missed it by one foot, and the other said we missed it by six inches.

FLYING THE SB-17 IN THE AIR RESCUE SERVICE

The SB-17 started its career in Air Rescue towards the end of World War II, when someone thought of the great idea of carrying a lifeboat underneath the fuselage and dropping it via a parachute to the survivors. The B-17 was a solid citizen in the long range category, it was proven and dependable, and most of all, available in large numbers.

My experience in the SB-17 was limited to a little over 100 hours, most of which was in the right seat as co-pilot. The hours I did fly from the left seat were mostly for taking an instrument check or a kindly instructor pilot letting me make some landings. It was strange to take the annual instrument check in a plane you weren't qualified to pilot, but the instrument check was given in the plane the instructor pilot was qualified to fly. But once you get airborne and set up in the area for the instrument check, the SB-17 flew like all the rest on instruments [and a little better I might add].

The lifeboat fit underneath, covering the bomb bay doors with the boat form fitted to the belly. It was pulled up tight against the fuselage and was directly connected to the bomb shackles in the bomb bay.

The boat was not heavy, but the drag contributed to a loss of airspeed during cruise. Without the boat, which normally was only installed for genuine sea searches, the SB-17 flew like a Piper Cub! It was smooth, predictable and handled very easy for a heavy aircraft. Had the plane possessed power controls, it would have been a plane you would have wanted to take home to introduce to your mother!

As I remember my first flight inside an SB-17, I didn't log any pilot time. Instead, I was given a pair of binoculars and placed in the tail gunners position to see if that was a good spot to take a close look at a 'sighting' on the ground. I figured at the time, and nothing has happened to change that opinion, that the assignment to the tail position was a form of hazing to put that new 2nd Lieut. in his place. Maybe to get me airsick, but no I didn't get sick and the surprise was that I could lock onto a small object with the binoculars when they were in a turn that pivoted the object. Of course, I could have seen the same thing from the waist gunner's position and not get grease on my pants getting into position to use the glasses. The SB-17 tail wheel retracted into the fuselage and it was a tight path to get past it to get into the tail gunner position.

I remember one flight as a co-pilot with an 'old timer' instructor pilot in the left seat. We were off on a functional check flight, so the plane was light and only three of us on board - including the flight engineer [crew chief] that was going to do the serious part of recording the engine readings. Lieut. Lothar completed the engine run-up and asked me to get us clearance from the control tower. They gave the clearance for takeoff and we lined up with the active runway. The pilot advanced the throttles gently and I followed to make sure they didn't slip back. I was busy checking the engine rpms and manifold pressure – 48 inches of MP was set, and we quickly gathered speed. In a short time, we were going fast enough to lift off, but we were still in contact with the runway. The pilot called out "Gear up!" I knew we were on the ground and looked down at the right wheel. The strut was moving up and down with the uneven cement and I turned to look at him.

He shouted, "God Damn it! I said gear up!"

What the hell, it wasn't my airplane, I reached up to the landing gear switch, lifted the guard, and raised the switch. Looking ahead, the hurricane perimeter fence was dead ahead and we were still at the same height. The gear retracted and he held the altitude! Finally, at what I thought was a tad too late, he eased back the control wheel and we cleared that fence with a small margin, and once past the fence, increased the back pressure on the control wheel and we zoomed to a climb attitude not usual in the 17. (After all, we were at March Field, California, the home of the 1st Fighter Group flying the new P-80s. Somehow you have to show you have style and pizzazz).

The B-17 had a unique landing gear and engine combination that allowed it to back up. There were no reverse pitch propellers [at least on the B-17], but with careful attention to detail, a pilot could back into the parking position. Consider that the B-17 had conventional landing gear, that is, two main gear and one tail wheel, a combination that lost favor in later years. This configuration allows turns by braking on one main gear wheel which would allow the tail to swing one way or the other to change direction. The outboard engines on the 17 were farther from the center of the plane than the main gear which in turn allowed the plane to turn by engine power assisting or alone. It is complicated to consider and not a natural way to maneuver an airplane.

For example, to back up the airplane, the pilot would first unlock the tail wheel so it could pivot freely, then hold the brake on the right wheel and increase the power of the No. 4 or right outboard engine, which would cause the left wheel to back up and the tail move accordingly [to the right in this case]. After a small turn 30 degrees or so, the pilot reduces the power on the right engine to idle, releases the right brake. He follows this by stepping on the left brake, and increasing the power of the No. 1 or left outboard engine. The nose moves to the right bringing the right wheel back. When the plane reaches the same number of degrees as the first turn and heading in the same direction, the plane has backed up a few feet. The backing up process can be continued until reaching the desired spot. As you can imagine it was not done often, but handy in the event there was no good method of taxiing into the parking spot.

In the cockpit photo, you can see the unique throttle construction. The throttles were painted green as I remember, but the ones in the photo are red, and it appears there are six handles. The arrangement allowed throttle selection of one or more throttles easy. Starting at the top of the throttle quadrant, the No. 1 and No. 4 are selected. The next levers down are split, each side left and right connected to an engine. The two halves on the left are connected to the No. 1 and No. 2 engines. The pair on the right connects to the No. 3 and No. 4 engines. This split lever arrangement allowed one hand to control all four throttles. The lower levers below the split throttles only controlled the No. 2 and No.3 inboard engines. Any of the sets of levers could be gripped palm up or palm down whichever you wanted in order to control both the left and right sides together.

FLYING THE L-5

The Operations Officer introduced me to the L-5 in 1948 upon arrival at Flight B, 4th Air Rescue Sqdn at March Field, CA. The L-5 was a WWII liaison airplane that served the Army well. As a newly minted 2nd Lieut., I was expected to learn some more about flying in the L-5 before taking on the more expensive airplanes like the SA-10 Catalina, C-47 Gooney Bird, and the SB-17 with the droppable lifeboat. It was OK by the other 2nd Lieut, Frank Johnson and me. The L-5 gave us the opportunity to fly by ourselves, make our decisions, and make our mistakes. There is a certain amount you learn in the right seat of a multi-engine plane, but the learning process is slow and greatly determined by the fellow in the left seat. If he makes too many really good decisions and doesn't explain them, you may miss the obvious, or if he makes the wrong decisions you end up with an undeserved feeling of superiority. So – if you fly alone and survive, you have accomplished a great deal – you develop self-confidence and tend to pay attention more when the engine is pulling you through the air.

First of all, the L-5 was a Stinson factory design, very similar to the Stinson 108 'Station Wagon' of the pre-WWII period. The 108 had side-by-side seating, but the L-5 was a two-seater tandem cockpit with lots of Plexiglas. The L-5 had a much bigger engine, pushing 190 horsepower and offering more performance. It was a light plane by the Air Corps standards, and not considered high tech or difficult. Besides, how much trouble could two Lieutenants get into while flying an L-5? As time passed, we found out, and much to our surprise we never had an accident that was reported.

The light weight and large engine in the L-5 made a good combination for search and rescue, and after some local flights for training and familiarization, we were off to the search areas when needed. Back in those days, a missing plane was not uncommon as the civilian flying was increasing rapidly, and bad weather always seemed to catch one of them trying to get somewhere. My memory is that during one year at Flight B, we had 300 'missions' processed. Some of them were short and quick, and some were extended.

We searched mostly mountainous terrain – It was Southern California after all – so Johnson and I got plenty of time and experience flying the 'contour' search, the search that starts at the top of the ridge or peak and continues downward. Dropping downward was an easy gig, but it was easy to get caught turning into a canyon. A couple of close calls of looking forward and seeing nothing but the side of a canyon was enough experience to make you more careful. And a good reminder to keep enough air speed to Chandelle out of trouble.

There were a few pilots that had the opinion that you could do a better job of searching by going slower, so they recommended flying with half flaps. The plane flew nice, more nose down, and a lot slower, but required a bit more power and there was very little reserve of air speed to get out of trouble. Both Johnson and I learned that the hard way.

We continued to build our experience, and both of us were on a constant quest to fly more than the other guy. We continually bugged the scheduling officer to let us fly. One day a large scale search came up, and they decided to send us both and solve the problem of trying to keep our flying hours even. It seemed a US Senator was in a missing plane up in Idaho, and they sent us to Lewiston in two L-5s; Frank carrying a mechanic with him, and I carrying the tools and baggage for all. As it happened, a staff officer, Capt Lyons, from the Rescue unit at Hamilton AFB was at March on a 'visit.' He was also flying an L-5, and he led the flight with Johnson and me on the wings. The L-5 had 4 hours of fuel and could probably go 300 plus miles before needing fuel, so the trip took a couple of days. Frank and I did get a lot of formation time, which we enjoyed and got to know this Captain Lyons and his flying methods and procedures pretty well. It boiled down to "expect anything to happen." We entered traffic and landed from a variety of positions and sometimes he brought us over the field to 'pitch out' for landing and sometimes not. It kept us on our toes and taught us not to expect the same thing twice. As a sidebar, we noticed he logged a couple more hours of flying on the trip than we did. . .hmm.

During one of the downtimes on the way to Idaho, Captain Lyons briefed us on various methods of searching in the mountains. He was one of those advocates of flying with half flaps to improve the searching. We arrived at Lewiston late in the afternoon, so we got settled in a motel for the night. In the morning, we were up early to go to the airport, brief, and head out to our search area. This search was a large scale operation that included all six of the west coast Rescue L-5s, Civil Air Patrol, and a few military units. Johnson and I were assigned areas close to each other, so we stayed together until reaching them to provide a little mutual support. The area was mostly trees and should we go down we would disappear like the object or our search. Both of our areas were the typical mountainous forest, some steep slopes and nearly solid with trees. We were looking for anything out of the ordinary – broken trees, shiny objects – anything out of place or didn't belong there. The plan was to fly out of Lewiston and recover for fuel and lunch at an advanced base. All six of the Rescue L-5s used this field and normally would come back for fuel about the same time.

I started out searching with half flaps and found it working OK; flying slow and holding the airspeed with the power, adding power in the turns, and backing off again in level flight. Reaching the end of the area, we started a descent turning away from the mountain side and turning back at the next altitude. Actively searching by almost continual looking out the left or right side and front while flying the plane added to the workload. It worked out fine for an hour or so. Later in the flight I was in a new section, starting at the top and had made a couple of trips at lower and lower altitudes. I didn't realize I had turned into a shallow 'valley' and as I flew to maintain my track, I was flying over slowly rising terrain looking out of the left window. I could feel the controls getting mushy at the slower speed and instinctively added power, but the plane didnt accelerate and the controls continued to be slack. A quick check of the airspeed confirmed I was getting pretty slow, and the plane was close to the tree tops. Starting a slow right turn away from the high ground, I added power, only to find that the throttle was already at the stop. I played with the fuel mixture to see if I could coax another 50 RPM from the engine. Sorry about that --- we were maxed out. Mister L-5 was in real slow-flight in a right turn, flying just above the stall. Looking forward and to the right, I could see two huge trees sticking out of the forest ahead in the path of the turn. Can't tighten the turn or I would stall. Can't loosen the turn or I will be flying into the trees on the high side. I chose to put the wing between the trees and hope for the best. We went through without touching and continued the turn until headed downhill, staying close to the tree tops to pick up speed. Once over the river, I settled down for a quiet smoke while I thought about the business of using the flaps during the search.

By the time I finished the cigarette and mashed it into the ashtray, I decided that the flaps would stay up, and went back to finish the section. At the end of that flight with the fuel low, Johnson and I met up again and flew to the advanced base for fuel and something to eat. This small field served as the mid-day recovery base for fuel, lunch and a discussion with the search base about your last mission and briefing for the next. After landing, I noticed the mechanic with Johnson working at the tail near the tailwheel. The mechanic explained that he was removing some tree branches from the mechanism! Frank Johnson had also gotten bit by the half-flap routine, and I could see that he got more 'experience' than I did.

We both agreed that we would keep the flaps up in the search area from then on. The second search flight went like the first, except we were more careful and kept the flaps up. After the second flight, it would be the end of the day and we would recover at Lewiston again. The search continued for several days, flying out of Lewiston, landing for fuel and lunch at the advanced base. The search covered all of the areas two or three times by a large number of aircraft, including the Civil Air Patrol, with negative results. Finally, one day we found out when we landed at the advanced base that our part in the search was suspended.

We sat around for a relaxed lunch waiting for the last plane to land, and we got into a discussion of when and how to return to Lewiston. Captain Lyons was the senior officer, and he decided, after listening to a lively discussion, that we should all go back together in formation! Some pilots liked it, some did not, but Johnson and I was for the formation. Lyons briefed the positions and how we would approach the field in a 'box' formation of two three ship Vs, and then when near the airport, change to the echelon for the overhead approach to landing. I had the number 2 position next to Lyons in the lead, with Johnson and three others down the line.

Once lunch was finished, planes refueled and the bills paid, we all went to our planes. After takeoff, the formation was joined and the two Vs forming the 'box' proceeded to Lewiston. Johnson and I were familiar with Captain Lyons formation and the unexpected consequences, so we were very alert for anything. *Anything did happen* as it turned out. The formation approached Lewiston from the East, prepared to land towards the West, the same direction as takeoff that morning. Lyons signaled us into the echelon formation to the right, with all the wingmen out to the right and slightly behind. I flew a position below his level to be able to see him in the cockpit, and the others followed suit, forming a pretty good looking echelon 'stacked down' slightly. Unfortunately, as we got closer to the field, it was apparent that the wind had changed so that now we were now coming in downwind. I saw that and started to figure out all of the possible things he could do to fix this problem. Take the formation away and come back into the wind, break up now and make individual downwind legs, etc., etc. No, nothing like that.

Lyons quickly devised a new 'pitch out to landing' and gave me the twirling finger to signal a break for landing. I passed this on to Johnson on the right, and the others relayed beyond.

We were at the downwind end of the field at about 500 feet, nearly over the runway intending to land in the other direction. Lyons looked back, nodded his head, and sharply peeled off to the left and down. I was determined not to lose sight of him and started a roll to the left and closed the throttle to stay with him and yet continue to get separation from the plane. This 'fan' pitch-out is pretty to watch when it is done well. I was to find out later that we did just fine. Lyons flaps came down to full as I watched his airplane and the runway in the background, almost straight below me. Dropping full flaps as soon as I could and kicking the rudder to add drag helped from running over him. I managed to stay behind him at a safe distance but didn't have time to check on Johnson behind me. The runway rushed up to Lyons and me, and we almost flared as a single unit, landed on the main gear and coasted to a taxi speed, still very close to him. During the turn to the taxiway, I looked back to see the other four L-5s close behind me! I felt pretty good about that, and later we congratulated ourselves [to an extreme] about our prowess as formation pilots!

It didn't work out too well for Captain Lyons though since the airport manager got to him quickly and chewed him out for the acrobatics that he just saw. He told Lyons: 'Some of these students will kill themselves thinking they can do that stuff !' 'You had six of those planes on the runway with the tailwheels off the ground at the same time !' 'That is too close together!' 'Don't do that again.' And other angry things. I understand that he later told someone else 'It looked pretty sharp.'

Once we got back into the operations building, the search commander told us that our part of the search was suspended because a Navy P2V was down near Vancouver Island. We were to leave immediately for McChord AFB to proceed on the search for the Navy plane. We scrambled to get our clothes and B-4 bags from the motel and back in the air. We proceeded to McChord and was stuck there for several days due to weather before we headed out for the Naval Station at Tofino on Vancouver Island. The trip was uneventful, except for the fact that I noticed the engine seemed to vibrate more while we were over water north of Port Angeles. Yeah, right. Of course, pilots new to flying over water always notice the engines are running rough.

The search out of Tofino was a routine search mission, with our part in the L-5s kept over the deep forest that exists. We were there about ten days, but the weather only allowed us to fly two days. As I recall, the wreckage of the P2V was found well north of our area, and we were released to go home. I took a few days for the weather to improve enough to allow these VFR aircraft to fly back to McChord.

Once at McChord we were released to return to March AFB, but the weather was still a problem. Johnson and I were at the weather station as often as we could go, bugging the forecaster for a good forecast. The ceilings were going up and down, barely reaching the VFR requirements at one place, but below somewhere else along the route. The ceilings seemed like an undulating rug stretched between Eugene, OR, and McChord, near Tacoma. By the third day, the forecaster was so tired of us even he was rooting for good weather to get rid of us. Finally, it happened. All of the stations between Eugene and Tacoma forecast, yes, VFR weather for a short period. We launched ASAP. We traded off being the lead in the formation, and this time it was my turn.

The weather was marginal, but we were satisfied to fly low as long as we were heading south to home. But the weather did get lower than VFR but the visibility seemed OK, so we kept going. Finally, we reached a river that appeared to be on course for most of the way to Eugene, and we stuck to that like glue. The visibility was miserable mainly reduced by rain. I tried to verify there were no power lines across the river, but it was difficult to read the map while flying so low and still frantically looking for things stretched across the river. I kept waiting for Johnson to suggest we turn around, but he didn't. He was waiting for me to call the turn back to McChord. Eventually of course we got to a position that going back would be more dangerous than continuing. My best memory is that we continued down the river for 40 or 50 miles at 200 to 300 ft. ceiling and one-half mile visibility. We were an accident waiting to happen. After 30 minutes or so at this very low altitude, frantically sticking to that river, the visibility SUDDENLY improved and within 5 minutes we were flying in partial sunshine. Sunshine ! We hadn't flown in weather this good in a long time! Break out the sunglasses! The best part was that Portland was just up ahead, and Eugene not far beyond. It felt good to get the rubber on the runway I can tell you. Johnson probably felt even better since his life was being used as a pawn against the elements by another 2nd Lieut. ! ! [The mechanic was in worse shape. He had no control nor said what happened, and he was at the mercy of the judgment of two 2nd Louies!]

Once on the ground we contacted the base, and they informed us to stay where we were. There was another airplane down, and the planes are going to that search. They quickly continued to say that two other pilots and a mechanic were coming up to fly the planes, and we would return home. Wow ! We were going home at last. Today was about the 30th day away from March AFB, and we were running out of clean clothes and money. The next day the squadron's C-47 arrived with two pilots and a mechanic, and we climbed into the passenger compartment and slept most of the way to March AFB.

The L-5 continued to provide the thrills and self-inflicted terror until I transferred from the unit.

Johnson and I adapted our ways to entertain ourselves and perhaps to outdo the other. We made steep climbing takeoffs to 300 ft. before the plane stalled. Also, we developed a 360-degree overhead approach in a partial stall, that should have ended in an accident. The procedure was to approach the short runway at cruise speed and over the touchdown point, close the throttle and roll into a left bank. Then pull hard on the stick to make a tight turn and slow the plane. The L-5 was soon rapidly losing altitude in the turn and airspeed reduced close to stall speed. At some point in the turn and speed reduction, air started flowing through the wing slots. The slots improved the stall characteristics, but the slow speed meant there was not enough elevator authority to raise the nose for the landing flare. A quick blip of the engine was enough to raise the nose and stop the airflow through the slots. You were 'flying' again and under control. Raise the nose enough to put the wheels on the runway and the landing 'made'. One day a new Captain in the unit, the new operations officer, saw both of us pitch out for landing and thought we were going to crash. He ran out and jumped in his car, but saw that we were taxiing in when he got beyond the buildings and could see us. Captain Halsey came down pretty hard on us, and we promised not to allow the wing to stall in the pattern anymore. Although after he had got proficient in the L-5, I saw him make one of those approaches. . . . just had to try it.

The slots in the wings worked great, removing any tendency for the wing to drop during the stall, but you could get into trouble with it in other ways. One fine day I was given the job of flying to one of the civilian airports for some publicity thing I can't remember, and I asked a friend to go along. Lieut. Griffin flew RF-80s in one of the recon squadrons but this was a Saturday and not much going on there. He agreed to go along for the fun of it, and the implied possibility that we would meet some movie starlet or two. The flight to the airfield was routine, but upon arrival I could see that a road ran very close to the end of the active runway. Not wanting to make a dragging approach over the traffic, I elected to make a slow steep approach.

It looked good there for a bit, but I didn't realize the wings were stalled. The airflow through the slots has disguised the stall, leaving us with very little lift and not able to flare the plane for landing. The plane hit the runway in the landing attitude but a stiff rate of sink. We heard Blam, no BLAM as the thing hit, and we bounced. I added power and made a go around, Looking at the landing gear it was easy to see the left tire was flat. The right one was OK, but the damage was done. I used one of the message streamers to drop a note telling them we were returning to March. As you can imagine, Griffin in the back seat was disappointed. He wasn't worried so much about getting killed when we had to land the plane, but he was very embarrassed to be in this little kite while an accident was going to happen. What a razzing he would take when they found out in the squadron! He moaned all the way back to March, complaining about being in this crate, and me asking him to go with him!

As it turned out, March had two runways and a pretty good breeze down the main runway. A landing on the crosswind runway with the wind on the right would cancel some of the left turning tendency of the flat tire. A careful and slow landing on the right wheel worked out just fine with the L-5 turning just 30 to 45 degrees towards the flat tire before stopping. A successful landing! But no, it wouldn't work out that way. The Airdrome Officer of the Day was a classmate, also in one of the fighter squadrons, came out to the runway to take charge. The plane was sitting on the flat tire but otherwise looked like a regular L-5. Lieut. Breitkreutz was of the opinion that he should report it as a major accident. His opinion was that the tire is a major part of the airplane, and the plane can't fly without it. Hmm That worried me because I was afraid that others would feel the same way!

About this time the mechanics from the Rescue unit came with a tug and towed the L-5 back to the hangar. Having nothing else to do, the AO took us to the officer's club. There we analyzed and re-analyzed both the first and the second landings several times over, with special attention to my lack of aviation skill and application. During the discussion, I called the maintenance section to ask if there was additional damage. The mechanic told me that they took the wheel off and replaced it with a replacement. When they separated the two halves of the wheel, they found the tube squeezed between the two halves of the wheel. Such good news I didn't deserve. So the blame for the blown tire was shifted to the rubber tube! My friends didn't believe me and insisted that I bought off the maintenance people. . . .

Search missions brought out the most interesting situations. Besides turning into a blind canyon, you could get sucked in by a bad assumption.

During one search mission for a downed airplane near Tehachapi, CA we operated out of the local airport. After the first mission, a deputy sheriff asked the search commander if he could fly as a scanner and suggested he knew the terrain very well. The search commander approved and introduced him to me. When I asked him if he knew the mountainous areas north of the town, he said he knew all this area 'like the back of his hand.' The weather wasn't the best for searching in the mountains, and we had to improvise to do any searches at all. Clouds obscured the mountain peaks leaving many of the saddlebacks open. I flew through one too many saddlebacks and tried to find the way out. We had been in the air 3 and a half hours, and it was getting dark. I had the impression from my memory of where we had been that the sun was setting in the East. ! I knew that was wrong, and I asked the deputy how to get back to Tehachapi.

He said, " Hell! I've never been here before !" With that, I decided to believe the compass and proceed westward and south through the passes to at least get to the valley. I could see there was no nice pasture here! The fuel by now was getting very low and became a major concern. I leaned the mixture a little more. With some luck, I arrived out of the mountain area over the highway to the valley, but how far was an airport? The pain in my gut wasn't from hunger as I turned to fly east towards Tehachapi and away from the valley area. The fuel gauge was very low, so I started rocking the wings to make sure all of the fuel was moved around to the outlet. I switched tanks a few times to make sure I was burning that fuel, and it gave me something to keep busy while I looked for the town of Tehachapi. It was full dark now, and I flew above the highway to avoid hitting anything. Finally the town lights showed, I switched tanks, rocked the wings, leaned the mixture for the umpteenth time, and said a prayer. I kept what altitude I had, and as the lights of the field could be made out, I reduced the power and started a fuel sipping descend to the runway. The landing was firm but felt like a grease job to me. The deputy was glad to get on the ground [and didn't volunteer to fly again]. The search commander asked me to explain why I was the last one on the ground and getting in after dark. He was afraid of having a second search mission on his hands.

The actual good news, thru no effort of mine, was that they found the missing plane and one passenger was alive but hurt very bad, and suffering from frostbite. Not many of our search missions concluded with a live survivor.

FLYING THE AIR FORCE L-13

The L-13 was a short-lived liaison aircraft in the late forties. It appeared to be spawned as a combination search aircraft and likely bush aircraft. It was designed to be folded up and put inside a cargo aircraft and carried to where it would go to work. The cabin was strange in those days, very wide, maybe wide enough to carry two to four barrels of fuel oil. There were two sets of pilot controls. Aft of the cabin, the fuselage shrank to what appeared to be a small aluminum tube, connected to a high elevator The plane was designed by Stinson, but built by Convair to some specs that I am not aware of, but there was a need for replacement of the WWII liaison planes and this was one of the answers.

The landing gear, as can be seen, is of the conventional or tailwheel type. One of the oddities that I remember was the brakes. The brakes were the same as the brakes on the L-5, a much lighter liaison plane. As it turned out, the brakes were so ineffective, they could not lock up the wheels on landing. "A good thing" eh? Don't want a lot of blown tires do we? Of course, being a tail wheel type configuration, it was necessary to have good brakes to keep control of the plane on the ground! Our Ops Officer, Major George Halsey made some tests by landing with the parking brake on. They were 'short' landings, but no blown tires, no flat spots. Of course, the smaller brakes couldn't hold the wheel from turning because the L-13 was heavier. One story at the time was that the smaller brakes were directed by the Air Force because there were a lot of them.

One of the interesting side issues with the aircraft was the placement of the pitot tube, the device that measures the impact air and static pressure for the air speed and the altimeter. Since the wings were designed to fold for transportation, the pitot tube couldn't be placed in the wing, the location of choice for a single engine plane. So it was stuck on top of the cabin and reached well above the prop-driven air [prop wash]. This was convenient only if someone else climbed up and removed the pitot cover that protects the pitot tube from bugs and other debris.

Note – I should add at this point that I did leave a cover on one day when in a great hurry and didn't notice the big red flag hanging down from the mast. I had flown the plane earlier in the day, but some neat freak had replaced the cover. I was surprised after takeoff when there was no airspeed shown on the indicator, in fact, showed a slight negative value. The result was a very careful traffic pattern and final approach. One of the best landings I ever made in the L-13.

The biggest shortcoming of the L-13 was the engine. Someone selected the Franklin O-425 putting out 245 hp to power the plane. The engine was equipped with a controllable pitch propeller which allowed high RPM [and power] for takeoff and low RPM [and economy] for cruise. To our surprise at the time, the prop blades were made of wood! In order to get the power they needed, the low pitch at takeoff resulted in 3500 RPM, a very high pitched 3500 RPM. It sounded like the sound you expect just before the engine explodes. Even in cruise, the RPM was a high pitched 2800 or so.

During the short history of the L-13, the airplane probably experienced more engine failures than one would expect, and without any statistics to back it up, I suspect it had the highest failure rate of any Air Force aircraft. Our unit at March Field, Calif. experienced a few, but others all over the Air Rescue Service did as well. At one point, the restrictions on flying the aircraft permitted flight only over terrain that you could expect a successful forced landing. Great confidence in the engine. This restriction came late in the short life of the L-13. Because of the restriction, a short time later the plane was taken out of service. Before the restrictions, we had a lot of adventures in the aircraft.

Check out in the L-13 was interesting, since the aircraft was new and some new wrinkles were introduced. The controllable pitch propeller was a new one to me. It was controlled electrically with a simple three position switch spring loaded to center. The switch changed the mechanical setting of the propeller blade. After the new pitch was selected the prop was like any other fixed pitch propeller. The fuel was loaded in the wings, a serious problem because the wings folded for transportation. The wing flaps were an unusually large and deflected 60 degrees. They were operated electrically, and the high amount of drag from the flaps allowed very steep approaches. In many respects, the L-13 gave the impression of an aircraft hastily designed and built by amateurs.

This impression is the strongest when you looked at the instrument panel. The plane was probably not designed to fly on an instrument flight plan since the instrument panel was laid out with little regard to the standard grouping of flight instruments.

The first few hours were getting used to the plane with a lot of landings, slow flight, stall recoveries, and steep turns – uh, how steep can you bank and not lose altitude? Short field landings were the most fun since the poor brakes weren't heavy enough to cause tire damage. The plane did well on short field takeoffs as well, with a willingness to lift off early. The technique that was settled on was to add full power, then release brakes and immediately apply full forward elevator to raise the tail. As soon as the tail came up to level, the control wheel could be brought back to raise the nose and lift off. It was impressive indeed after flying the L-5! The full flap landing was a very steep approach and as the nose came up for landing the airspeed disappeared quickly. A 'good' landing required only one fast flare to get the nose up and an immediate stall just above the runway. A smooth landing was nearly impossible, as the plane sank immediately upon reaching the landing attitude. No fishing for the runway. If you were at 3 feet when the landing attitude was reached, the plane fell three feet - simple as that.

One day a classmate flew with me to see what it was like. He, like others on the other side of March Field, flew F-80s or RF-80s. We flew in the traffic pattern and I demonstrated some 'good' landings [mostly] made with various amounts of flaps and made the last one full flaps. It was 'ok' [lower case] and I offered him the plane to try a landing. I knew he would blow it and I would be able to hold it over his head for the rest of his life. He proceeded to take off, make a fair pattern and turned final. He extended full flaps, and pulled the power off and pointed the nose to the end of the runway. The plane came down like it was on an elevator shaft. I was ready to take over and thought he wasn't going to pull the nose up and started to reach for the control wheel. He pulled back and the nose came up. I thought we were going to hit, but he stopped the rate of sink and the wheels rolled onto the runway! I muttered something about a lucky landing and he refused to make any more. They wouldn't be any better than that.

The L-13 design turned out to be a good search platform. The windows were slanted outward to give good visibility and the nose design provided a low nose profile giving good visibility forward. The plane was two people wide, in fact, contained four seats, but our unit was seldom equipped to fully man or even provide two people. The result was to adjust the search patterns so you covered everything from the left side and adjusted the tracks accordingly. One of our early searches using the L-13 was a search for two F-80s in Arizona that were missing following a night training flight. The squadron was alerted for the mission but held after we assembled the aircrews while they tracked down leads. They alerted two of us to fly our planes to Phoenix and perform the search. The search commander was in a third airplane. We launched for Williams Field at 3 or so in the morning after waiting for confirmation,. The flight was a good 3 hours since the L-13 was not too speedy. The word fast did not appear in the flight handbook. So we got there at dawn and after a quick briefing and a cup of coffee, we launched to the most promising search area. By this time, the belief was that a mid-air had occurred and the two jets would be close together.

Two of us flew our L-13s out to the assigned areas. The terrain was flat, desert without any real navigation check points, but we were going slow and could see the ground well beyond the next search leg. I was getting sleepy at the same time, and staying awake was a continuing effort. By this time I was awake for over 24 hours, and while I had done 'that' before, being in the airplane at low altitude was a first. As I got more and more sleepy, efforts to stay awake alternated between opening the window to stamping my feet and slapping my legs and face. As it turned out, the effort to keep looking out the window searching kept me awake on the straight search legs, but the turns back to the reverse heading was a chance to rest. I would 'kind of' rest or relax during the turns and perk up in time to roll out of the turn and get back to business. That worked for a while, but eventually I woke up at very low altitude going in the original direction! Full throttle, pull back on the wheel and get back to the search altitude. That scared me enough to provide the adrenalin to keep me awake the rest of the flight.

At the end of that mission, the other L-13 pilot and I got a quick bite to eat while they were refueling the planes and launched again. The second mission was cut short when we received the radio call to return to base. Both F-80 wreckages were located well south of us. We returned to Williams AF Base, went to the Visiting Officers Quarters and slept.

Quite unconnected to the L-13 flight, my squadron commander, Major Helmick, was a friend of the Major that headed the Acrojets, the forerunners of the Thunderbirds. He prevailed on him to get me a ride in a TF-80, the two-seater made to provide a second cockpit. This plane was later called the T-33. The flight went well, although uneventful as far as anything unusual, but it made an exciting flight for me. Major Helmick bought a lot of loyalty out of that action to get me that ride. I was determined to get into jets, but it took a long time before I managed it. That first flight was in 1949.

One search mission took place in Utah. A civilian airplane was down northeast of Las Vegas. The squadron launched our aircraft to the area, and I got one of the two L-13's. The mission was being run out of an airport near Cedar City, UT. Fortunately for me, I had a mechanic along riding in the right seat during the mission.

On the very first flight from the main search base to the search area, about an hour into the flight, the engine started running rough – missing actually – and it lost power. I turned to go back to the search base and started working the engine rpm and airspeed to maintain level flight. The best it would do was a slow descent. The engine was laboring, and we couldn't reach anything close to full rpm. We found a highway leading to the airport and followed it closely. The slow descent brought us down to within 200 ft. or so of one of the saddle backs we had to go through. After that, the terrain fell off, but we maintained as much altitude as possible. We limped into the airport and landed, with the engine running very rough after the power was reduced for taxiing.

The mechanic checked the engine very carefully. There was a lot of oil in the engine compartment, which was cleaned off thoroughly. Oil was found in the magnetos and the oil got into the points, which caused the misfiring. By the late afternoon, they had cleaned all the oil out of the engine and magnetos, and test run the engine. No oil was found leaking on the engine run-up and the plane was released for flight. I was assigned another search area and took off when the plane was ready.

As it happened, about an hour into the flight the engine roughness returned and before the power got down too low, we headed back to the search base. The engine was suffering when we arrived, but it was still running well enough to fly at the pattern altitude. Again the mechanic found oil in the engine compartment and in the magnetos. He cleaned the oil from the engine and magneto again and declared the plane ready. The mission commander though, thought that we would be better off if I flew the plane to the Hill Air Force Base at Ogden, Utah, get the thing fixed properly and after that get back to the search. They sent another mechanic with me to take care of any problems enroute, and we launched for Ogden. Hill AF Base was a major depot and clearly the place to go for some needed maintenance. Did they have L-13 parts? Not to worry, they could make them.

As we expected, at some time after departure, the engine started running rough again, and we were nowhere close to Ogden. We picked out a small airport ahead of us that looked close enough to reach and landed there. For the third time, we found oil all over the engine compartment and in the magnetos. Without the proper solvents, the mechanic had to innovate and came up with the idea of washing the magnetos out with the carbon tetrachloride fire extinguisher. He flushed out the magnetos and that about exhausted the material in the extinguisher. We wiped what oil we could off the engine and left the rest.

At this point, we were almost close enough to Ogden AF Base to make it without another shot of carbon tet. We launched out of there with Ogden as our destination, only altering the straight line by staying over ground we could make a forced landing if necessary. As the flight progressed, the engine once again started losing power, with a roughness that told us that the same thing was going to happen again. With the engine tone changing for the worse from time to time, we did manage to limp into the airport area. We made the obligatory call to the control tower that we had a problem and needed to land. Traffic was light and the tower cleared us to land on any runway. The wind was light and we chose the runway with the end closest to us and landed with the engine still running, but with too little power for level flight or a go-around. The landing was actually uneventful until the tail wheel rolled on the runway, and we could hear a rattling noise and I felt vibration or oscillation on the rudder pedals. In addition, the tower notified we had shed some parts on the runway and asked us to hold our position until the transient crew could come out and inspect the plane. We did as we were told and they came right out and picked up a few parts from the tail wheel, then approached the cockpit. The man advised us that he thought it was OK to taxi in slow and they would follow and pick up anything else that might come off [a little dark humor on his part]. We taxied in and turned over that clunker to the depot. They grudgingly accepted it. They had to, that was their job.

I sent a message to the home base advising of what happened to the plane and that we had turned it over to maintenance at the depot. I could visualize the sigh of relief that the plane was no longer their responsibility. We got a room at the Visiting Quarters for the night. A call to the mission base was not practical. In those days, the telephone was a luxury item and very few calls were made by us. I used the base message center through Base Operations and sent a TWX, [like a telegram] to our home base, but the mission base on the civilian field was not in the circuit. They knew where we were and the home base would brief them when they communicated the day's search results. The mechanic and I stayed overnight and were picked up by a plane from the mission base and returned to finish out the mission by filling in where we were needed until the search ended.

The L-13 was left at Ogden until it was repaired and someone else went up to fly it back a week or so later. The depot reported that the problem was caused by the rocker box covers being too thin. The rocker box covers are the metal plates at the end of each engine cylinder. The name Franklin stamped into the metal, which made the metal thinner at the edges of the letters. Eventually, the metal cracked, allowing oil to escape inside the cowling to be carried by the strong airflow to the rear. The oil flowed to the magnetos, got into the points insulating them. This affected one cylinder at a time until more cylinders were not firing. When the two spark plugs in the same cylinder didn't fire, the engine got rough along with the loss of power. At some point in the process, the power became insufficient to maintain altitude even at reduced speeds.

As time went on, the L-13 engine failures became a large burden and flying restrictions were imposed to prevent serious accidents. At one point, we were only allowed to fly over terrain that a successful forced landing could be made. That did put a squeeze on the flying schedule and almost eliminated any useful mission for the airplane.

I said goodbye to the L-13 by ferrying a couple to storage at Alameda Naval Air Station near Oakland. Most of the Air Force L-13s headed out that way and if all the stories could be told, it would be series of narrow escapes from making forced landings. In my case, the first one went to Alameda like it was a rented horse returning to the barn. No problem with the engine. [maybe we solved that problem after all]. No, on my next flight I was privileged to make my fifth forced landing in a total of 125 hours of flying the L-13. None of these landings were made dead stick, or no power at all, but in each case enough power was lost to prevent level flight.

For our second ferry flight, Lieut Ed LaDou and I were scheduled to take two L-13s up to Alameda. The flight started out normally in a loose formation and we drudged slowly up across the desert through Tehachapi Pass and headed out past Bakersfield and towards Fresno. As in the past, the engine started running rough [maybe 'missing' or limping is more correct]. I told LaDou of the problem and he crept in closer to look the plane over. We immediately started looking for an airport or a nice big field to land in if the engine got worse. There were no airfields in sight, only a wide expanse of barley fields.

These fields are worked much like rice, in that the field is flooded to grow the barley. Roads or work lanes were elevated around each field, but 'very' narrow. Lt. LaDou offered some advice on fields he could see. It didn't take long before I reached the point where I couldn't slow the plane any more in order to maintain altitude and started a slow descent. Now, it looked like I could visualize the maximum distance I could 'milk' out of this descent. There is nothing out there but barley fields. Some had water in them and some did not. That narrowed down the desired landing places considerably, and as the altitude got lower, I could finally pick out three fields that I could reach – and one looked very wet. I picked the nearest of the 'dry' fields and told Ed that I had the field dead ahead. He came back with "By the way, you look like you are on fire."

I answered, "Thanks a lot." [not much conversation in those days, you had to have the mike in your hand to talk. Push to talk was a ways off.]

My final into the 'dry' field got tighter as the power diminished and the sink rate increased. Instead of aiming for the first third of the field that

I wanted, it looked like I would be short! That meant that I would be landing into the raised dike. On short final, I could see the touchdown point was the base of the dike, and in desperation, hit the flap switch for an instant. The plane lifted over the dike and then started a second sink into the field. It was mud! I flared the plane to bring the nose up and get the speed as slow as possible and turned off the mag switch. We hit tail wheel first. The plane 'rolled' about a plane length and a half and started to nose over when the main wheels dug in. We stopped and the plane settled back in the three-point position. I jumped out with the fire extinguisher to see if I needed to put out a fire, but there was no fire. The oil had been getting on the exhaust and the smoke looked like fire to LaDou.

I got back in and called Ed, told him we were OK. He said he would report my position to Airways, and went on his way to Alameda. Airways in those days were the military version of Flight Service, handling flight information, weather, and passing clearances. As it turned out Ed got to Alameda in good shape without a lot of oil ruining his cross country.

Back outside the plane I looked it all over to see if we were without any dents, and while I was doing this, a fellow drove up in a pickup. He walked through the mud and introduced himself and told me he heard the strange noises from the engine and wondered if I was OK. We discussed the problem of the plane in the field of mud and how we were going to get the plane up on top of the dike and onto the road. He said he came prepared and together we hooked up a long rope to the tail wheel. Then, using the truck, he pulled it up onto the road! The miracle of miracles, this farmer had an airplane and a strip right on this piece of land I landed on. Without so much as a shrug, he anchored the tail wheel to the bed of the pickup and very carefully towed that hummer to his strip. I couldn't believe it and couldn't stop expressing my good luck for picking his field to land in.

The good luck continued, as that night he had a meeting to attend and invited me along as his guest. He was a member of the King County Sheriff's Aero Squadron. I quickly called the Airways people and explained my situation. They were already aware of my problem from Ed LaDou and were working on getting through to the squadron.

By the time we were ready to go to his meeting that evening, the squadron had already made plans to pick me up the next morning at Bakersfield. I should mention that back in 'those days' we seldom flew in flying suits, in fact, I am not sure I had an actual flying suit in 1949. I should mention that back in 'those days' we seldom flew in flying suits, in fact, I am not sure I had an actual flying suit in 1949. Maybe I did, but seldom used one, so I was already wearing the pink pants and brown Ike jacket and chukker boots, so I was ready to go anywhere. The evening was great, met a lot of friendly faces and basked in the glow of newly rescued airman after a close call. The highlight was the dinner of crab [the first I had ever had, and tasted great] and wine from a goatskin bag.

The idea of drinking from a goatskin bag is to drink from the nozzle at the end. You start with the nozzle near the mouth and as you squeeze to make the wine flow, you extend your arm to full length and back to your mouth. The goal was to not spill any wine on yourself. They did allow me to use a napkin on my jacket since I was dressed to the nines, but all of the others did it without a napkin. As it turned out, my napkin ended up clean as well.

FLYING THE PT 23

[file photo]

One sunny Saturday morning at March Field, California in 1949 my good buddy asked me to go flying with him. A quick trip, we would fly down to the farm of a friend of his where he could pick up his car, then I would fly his airplane back. His airplane was a war surplus PT-23 he had recently purchased and the thought of flying it sounded great.

Normally, both of us flew Air Force aircraft at March Field since we were both 2nd Lieutenants in the new Air Force. My friend (whom I'll simply call "Griff"), flew RF-80's in a recon squadron while I flew mostly liaison aircraft in the rescue squadron. It wasn't unusual for us to rent an aircraft on a weekend for fun, but Griff made the plunge and bought one.

Griff flew the PT-23 whenever he could; however what with the airplane and car and other expenses, there wasn't an awful lot of money left for fuel - the airplane or the car. As a result, Griff became very adept at fuel conservation (thirty years before everyone else) and was never known to have "topped off" the fuel tanks. His philosophy was to put in a half hours worth of fuel if he wanted to fly 30 minutes.

We arrived at the West Riverside airport where Griff added a few gallons of fuel to the right tank (all he could afford) and declared we were mission ready. After all, the trip to the farm was a very short one - just over the horizon.

Takeoff was normal, smoothly executed on the right main tire. The tire tread on the left wheel was a little thin [with 3 of the 4 plies showing] and Griff was making the thing last as long as he could. We carried a spare tire in the baggage compartment in case it was needed. During climb out the RPM was quite low, but I knew Griff was familiar with cruise climb techniques. Following level off, I noticed he moved the fuel selector to the left tank, and as I read the gauge in the wing, it was empty! In order to bring it to his attention, I casually pointed to the gauge (as casually as you might point to a burning engine). Griff gave me the universal "OK" signal. Presently, the engine sputtered, lost RPM, and he moved the fuel selector to the right tank, and the engine quickly smoothed out to its cruise setting. It dawned on me: "Of course, he was just burning off the slosh fuel in the empty tank so it wouldn't evaporate!" I sat back and relaxed, knowing that I was in the hands of a dedicated professional.

Letdown and landing in the farm field were uneventful. Fortunately, a series of small ridges of soil (used in irrigation) were lined up into the wind, and gave the pilot something to think about, and provided excellent motivation to stay in the three-point attitude. The PT-23 was turned around for takeoff, and I was ready to head back for West Riverside. Griff briefed me.

The briefing was thorough and covered several aspects of the flight (he thoughtfully omitted the time hack since the aircraft clock wasn't working anyway). The most important part of the briefing concerned FUEL CONSERVATION - a necessary and logical step since we didn't have much. He was an expert at saving fuel and he poured out all of his trade secrets. The gist of the briefing was this:

"....You have enough fuel to get back to West Riverside airport and make one go-around - providing you do what I say".

Just as soon as you start moving the throttle forward, release the brakes and put the stick to the right to save some wear on the left tire. Don't burn up fuel while you're sitting still. As you pick up speed, put the stick all the way forward to get the tail up as soon as possible. The "wing drag" from the wing moving thru the air in a 3-point attitude really eats up the gas. But, just as soon as the tail comes up, you start picking up "wheel drag" from the wheels rolling on the ground, and it's really sucking up the gas. Reach down and move the flaps to half and pull back on the stick. That gets rid of the wheel drag, but now you're in the air and rapidly increasing the "flap drag," and you know what flap drag does. Get rid of that flap drag by letting go of the flap handle (which was spring loaded), then as soon as you recover from the stall.... move the mixture back one inch. When you get rudder control, pull the power back 300 RPM, and when you feel the aileron control, start your turn out of traffic. Turn right, since it's closer (a 170 degree turn). Move the throttle back to the mid-point on the quadrant and climb to 2500 feet. At level off, throttle back to 1300 RPM, pull the mixture back until you lose 100 RPM."

"I know," I interjected for the first time, "then move the mixture forward until the 100 RPM is regained, which will avoid detonation."

"Wrong, you move the throttle forward to gain back the 100 RPM. Didn't Lindbergh teach you anything?" Griff replied, "There's no worry about detonation: the cylinders are right out there in the slipstream where they get maximum cooling."

I was too concerned with the immediate prospects of flight to question the details of the briefing. I was having trouble getting my scarf to stay on the outside of the cockpit and had no time for less urgent things. Besides, if I forgot something, I still have the reserve fuel he promised me to make that one go-around. Who needs to make a go-around in a plane that you can slip AND is equipped with flaps (and I'm secretly glad he told me about the flaps).

The takeoff proceeded, "normally" until about lift off when I had an overpowering urge to chandelle. Pulling up sharply to the left to circle the field one time, I rolled out on course with the vision of Griff shaking his fist at me. Climbing out with slightly conservative power settings (with respect to the briefing) towards West Riverside, I noticed a very stiff tailwind when I observed my ground shadow (Good, maybe I'll have that reserve fuel for the go-around after all).

Long before West Riverside was to loom out of the haze, the engine sputtered and lost RPM ("Damn, why did I get up today?"). Looking over the cockpit rim, the only flat spot visible was a highway packed bumper to bumper with traffic. Using panic induced logic, I was convinced that the tank still had some fuel in it, so I rocked the wings slightly and worked the hand pump rapidly. The engine caught roared to life and I started an immediate climb. The engine died a few seconds later, so the wing rock, hand pump routine was repeated. The engine caught a second time and a climb started again. The engine sputtered a third time, but by now the wing rock, fuel pump trick barely got a pop out of the windmilling engine.

While stretching the glide over the highway, looking frantically for a piece of level ground, the ground shadow of the PT was still moving rapidly. Still no place on the ground to put down the plane or even make a good crash landing. Suddenly, an airport (Arlington) appeared out of the dense haze, and lo and behold it was within gliding distance - but downwind. The prospect of a downwind deadstick landing was a sweetheart deal after considering the gullies beside the highway.

The tailwind was even stronger than I thought, so as I got closer, I could see that I could make the crosswind runway – unbelievably good fortune. As the glide continued with much luck (and some innate skill), I could see that the plane was able to reach the runway into the wind! With prop stationary, the deadstick landing was made into the wind exactly on the end of the runway. Fortunately, a turn-off appeared at the right time, and the old PT coasted nearly to the parking area. The driver of the small refueling truck drove over and asked what happened. I explained briefly that I ran out of fuel and was in a hurry to get to West Riverside airport.

"I could hear the engine cut in and out and wondered what was going on. Fill it up?" he asked.

"Nope, give me 5 gallons, " I replied, knowing the destination was just over the hill.

I tried leading my friend to believe I had crashed his PT-23 by leaving him a note telling him just the part about running out of gas and having to put it in a field [and suggesting that maybe there might not be any more use for the helmet and spare tire] (after all, both of us should learn 'something' from this experience).

Griff was a sad customer in the Officer's Club bar when I arrived later that night and when he saw me he sounded off several paragraphs explaining what he thought about my flying abilities and vented his disappointment in the crash.

Eventually, I confessed that the PT was in good shape and told the whole story in detail. Griff then spoke about my great flying skills and that he always had confidence I would not damage the PT-23. When the part was proudly related about the inspiration to use all of the slosh fuel, Griff didn't seem satisfied.

"What about the fuel in the left wing?" he asked

"The left wing tank was empty, you drained it on the way down to the farm," was my only logical reply.

Griff threw his cap down and exclaimed, "You mean that you risked a crash landing with my airplane when you had plenty of fuel in the left line?" What could I say?

THE DEMISE OF AN AIR MEDAL

Often in the discussion of medals and awards for military duties, there are stories of how one fellow got a lower award than others for doing the same thing. There are lots of stories of having an award send in by the commander for one award and having it lowered or downgraded to another level. It is a common ailment during combat, when the awards committees knock down the recommendations of the people in the fray...."Yeah, they put me in for the DFC but the jerks in Headquarters downgraded it to an Air Medal."

This story is not a combat story, however, it took place during the Korean War when awards were being given for non-combat efforts. The events took place a half world away from Korea in the skies of northern Canada.

....Goose Bay was 125 NM away and normally the low frequency radio could be heard. Not this time. The navigator rechecked and confirmed the heading was correct. Not too many minutes later we tried to retune to the Cape Harrison radio behind us on the Bendix. No joy. The set was silent except for the ever-present static. Through a break in the clouds we saw the lights of a small fishing village slip by. Little did we know that we would have welcomed the sight of them again later in the flight.

This all started one morning in mid-September 1951. Our squadron, the 52nd Air Rescue Squadron, was located at Ernest Harmon AFB, near Stephenville, Newfoundland. The base was part of the network of US bases covering that part of the U.S. and Canadian Northeast. Harmon was a refueling base for Military Air Transport planes, and provided the Rescue unit and some other support services for that part of the world.

The phone rang in the Squadron's rescue control center. The duty officer quickly picked up and said, "Harmon Rescue!"

A request came in from the Group headquarters that we dispatch a plane to pick up an ill Air Force officer at one of the many remote weather stations. This particular weather station was located on Padloping Island, just north of the Arctic Circle in the Northwest Territories and part of Baffin Island group. Baffin Island is west of Greenland and lies about the arctic circle [i.e. 66 deg. North Latitude]. Weather information in that Arctic area was important enough for the U.S. Air Force to assign up to seventy people to provide the weather analysis, communications, and the needed support people for housing, food, and off-time activities. Supplies and people coming in and going out were normally transferred by ship. However, the next supply ship was not expected before the harbor was filled with ice flow, putting off the arrival of the supply ship until spring. It was reported that the officer was suffering from an ulcer.

Major Jay Stansbury, the commander of 52nd Air Rescue Squadron decided to stage a plane out of Goose Bay, Labrador and position it there to refuel before the 20 – 22 hour flight out of Goose. The weather at the destination was questionable, and we would have to wait for the weather to break before proceeding to Padloping Island. The plane to be used was a no-brainer. A former Navy PBY called the SA-10 by the Air Force, would allow the water landing at Padloping Island and use the Goose airport for land operation. I was selected as the Aircraft Commander and he elected to send two other pilots, Lts. John C. Donahoe and James Huffman for relief in the cockpit. The three pilots were considered necessary, even before the days of the maximum duty time and crew rest rules put into effect in later years. The Navigator, Lt. Schlegel, a well qualified navigator with much over-water experience. The flight engineer, radio operator and radar operator rounded off the crew. In addition, a flight surgeon was added to care for the patient once we picked him up. We spent a couple hours working the navigation problems, fuel consumption, which were no small thing to a bunch of guys who hadn't been there before.

Most of us had been north of Goose Bay and had flown to Greenland and Iceland, but there had never been a need to go to Padloping Island. Padloping Island was one little island among a hundred others in the bigger area known as Baffin Island. The flight plan was going to be about 20 flying hours under average conditions and the need for VFR weather on the return to Goose Bay was important. We could go to Padloping Island and use Goose Bay for an alternate, but the return flight would not have enough fuel for an alternate airport.

The squadron possessed two SA-10's, and we chose the plane that carried the most fuel. Rubber tanks had been installed in the second SA-10 and the total fuel load was considerably less than the plane with the 'wet' fuel tanks. These tanks were called wet because the huge tank on each wing had only sealant at the seams to reduce the volume. The plane with the wet tanks could carry 1275 gallons of aviation fuel, and with a little luck it would last 22 to 24 hours. We noted a small refueling base at Frobisher Bay, about 3/4 the way to Padloping Island. It was only available as a seaplane base and had only a non-directional beacon for an instrument approach.

The PBY was a big airplane from the viewpoint of World War II. The wing was 104 feet from wing tip to wing tip and it stood tall. Our plane, the Air Force SA-10 was the PBY5A version, an amphibian design by Consolidated Aircraft. The plane we flew was made in Canada by Canso. The amphibian version added large wheels that extended from the fuselage. *These large main gear and the design of the wing standing on a tall pylon above the fuselage, made the plane high off the ground.*

The plane was awkward looking because of the high position of the wing and the two Pratt and Whitney R-1830 engines sitting far off the ground. The standard entry was up a metal ladder into the large Plexiglas enclosure observation point, called a blister, behind the wing on the left side of the plane. The right side had a blister too, as they were holdovers from the days when it was used as a side gunner position. We in Air Rescue Service used the large enclosures as great viewpoints for the observers during search and rescue missions.

Inside the SA-10 was outfitted very sparsely. Upon entering the blister from the ladder, you're in a large Plexiglas room, or so it seemed. Entering the watertight hatch to the inside of the plane it was obvious there was no interior insulation or 'upholstery.' One could see the green zinc chromate paint covering the metal interior that was used to ward off corrosion. The metal interior 'walls' were the same sheets of aluminum that served the outside of the plane. Narrow wooden walkways provided a means of moving around without stepping on the outside skin. This first interior room was a large room equipped with a canvas bunk on each side. Probably at one time, the space held two bunks per side. In the same area further forward, interior space was given up to the housing for the wheels and struts on each side of the fuselage. Passing this narrow point, there was a galley of sorts, including a hot plate and some limited storage. Looking up from the walkway [or catwalk] you looked up into the flight engineer's station.

The flight engineer sat on a seat suspended inside the pylon between the body and the wing. You could see some of the engine controls and gauges from down below. Just forward of the engineer's station, you went through another hatch into the radio and navigation positions. The radio operator occupied the right side with his equipment. Other radio equipment was located in racks forward of this point. The navigator occupied a table on the left side, with his loran set and other navigation instruments. He had the very accurate magnetic compass as well. The radar operator used a small area in front of the navigator's table where an old radar set was mounted. Finally, climbing up into the pilots'

compartment, you could slide into one of the pilot seats. The nose wheel compartment that held the retracted nose wheel was located immediately below the pilot positions. A small storage area was located forward of the pilot compartment along with access to the front hatch and the area formerly used by the front gunner to man a machine gun or a crew member to sight the bomb release during a bombing run.

Our SA-10 was serviced full up with fuel [1275 gallons of 110/130 fuel], oil [50 gallons of oil behind each engine], survival kits, Mae West floatation vests, C rations for in-flight meals, and we departed early afternoon for the 2 hour and 45 minute trip to Goose Bay .The nearly 300 nautical mile flight up was routine, a little weather, but nothing to worry about. We checked out all of the navigation equipment and found the plane operating great.

Navigation equipment was state of the art, as of World War II, requiring the navigator to work his magic. The plane was equipped with the 'new' loran system – the one that used a cathode ray tube for interpretation and took about ten minutes to determine where you were ten minutes ago. Of course there was bad news, when the navigator pointed out that the Loran was not precise in the area of the Northeast that we were headed. A technical factor in the design introduced errors in certain areas of the loran signal known as the Base Line Extension. The plane was equipped with two direction finding navigation radios; one of them was a powerful set made by Bendix that was very accurate. Unfortunately, the loop antenna used to find your bearing was turned manually. A second set was a radio that did a good job and was equipped with an Automatic Direction Finder [ADF] instrument needle, which continually attempted to show the bearing to the station. The frequency range of these radios was limited to the very low band for navigation stations and a second band for the AM broadcast band.

Upon arrival at Goose, we topped off the tanks and oil again and checked the weather. Weather information in those days was sketchy, based strictly on the various weather stations reporting their detailed information to all others. The Base Weather station's forecaster on duty analyzed these reports and made his own assessment of the conditions and his own forecast. The weather reporting stations in that part of the world were widely scattered and precise weather forecasts were not easy to make. On the other hand, I don't remember more busted forecasts in those days, despite working with teletype reports of weather formatted messages – mostly Greek to us pilots – and the forecasters did a credible job.

That said, the weather forecast for Padloping Island was not good enough for us to launch to take advantage of an early-morning arrival. The flight was going to be at least nine or 10 hours one way, maybe more, so it was important to start at night. So we went to bed about nine, checking with the forecaster every hour. The routine was get up, call weather, get the forecast, go back to bed, and then repeat every hour for five hours. The forecaster was a pleasant guy, understood the pressure of getting there, picking up the patient and getting back. The forecaster probably knew the officer at Padloping Island, since the patient was a weather officer also. Finally, after much discussion and disclaimers, the forecaster allowed that the weather was flyable. In the worst case, if we had to return without landing, the squadron could send up a fresh crew to fly the mission tomorrow. The route also afforded an emergency fuel stop at a place called Frobisher, a seaplane base with minimum services. We hoped that this fuel stop would not be necessary. A stop at Frobisher would add a lot of time to the trip, since the refueling operation would be very slow. We were looking at nearly 24 hours total including ground time, for the operation.

We woke everyone up around 2:30 or 3 o'clock and proceeded to the plane. I had catnaps between calls to the weather forecaster, but basically had not slept since six the morning before. Everyone was prompt in getting to the plane and we pre-flighted in the dark. Morale was good with the expectation of a big adventure ahead and the banter between the crew was jovial. Going to a destination like Padloping Island, an unprepared seaplane place, was exciting, but not foreboding. We checked with the crew in the rear of the plane to ensure they were ready and began going through the starting engines checklist. The coordination between the pilots and the engineer was not difficult; however the engineer had most of the controls to start the engines and the pilots had the throttles and magneto switches, plus the propeller controls. Once the engines were running and the fireguard on the ground waved us OK, we called Ground Control on the radio for taxi to the active runway. The engines tested good on the run-up and all equipment checked operational. The co-pilot called the tower to get clearance to take position on the runway, we eased into position on the active runway, made the last second check of the checklist items and pushed the throttles forward. With plenty of runway, we released the brakes and let the plane roll while the power was being advanced. Throttles push forward until the manifold pressure reached 42.5 inches of mercury and the engine speed set at 2450 rpm. Takeoff was a routine night takeoff, not too bad considering the heavy weight and the absence of lights off the end of the runway. As soon as the runway lights passed under the nose, it was like being stuck inside an ink bottle. Time to retract the landing gear - pull the safety button for the landing gear retraction handle and rotate the handle clockwise. The gear handle was located in front of the right knee of the pilot and handier for him to operate than the co-pilot in the right seat. The hydraulic system starts the landing gear to the UP position. We hear the nose gear snap into position and feel the thump of the big main landing gear wheels behind us settling into the up locks. No sweat, hold the attitude indicator five degrees nose up, stick the airspeed on 90 knots, keep the wings level and climb out. Once safely high enough to turn, we started a slow turn to the first checkpoint.

The SA-10, sometimes lovingly called the 'P BOAT,' had limited supercharging, so the top cruising altitude was about 12,000 feet, and lacking oxygen to use, we kept it mostly under 10,000, while the best range was around 6,000 to 8,000 feet altitude. The SA-10 was a high-drag device – part of the state of the art at the time. The wing was thick and developed a lot of lift and also a lot of drag. The high position of the wing kept the props out of the water spray on takeoff, but the round fuselage and pylon between the wing and body contributed to a very unstable heading in cruise. The nose of the plane moved through a flat horizontal figure eight, called a Dutch Roll that was very annoying. The pilot flying the plane was always on the rudder pedals to keep the heading reasonably solid. It was not a stable instrument airplane, but it did have one of the gyro-operated autopilots, which did a reasonable job [still with the little wiggle]. The control surfaces on the wings and tail were probably larger than if the plane was strictly a land plane. Once on the water, the SA-10 needed huge control surfaces for drag to help steer while taxiing, using the wind and the prop wash to get the very most control. As a result, the mechanical job of flying the SA-10, moving the huge surfaces to maneuver, required more muscle than most planes of that day. As I recall, each aileron of the SA-10 had about the same area as one Piper Cub wing.

We found ourselves in the clouds early in the climb and we fought the plane through the light turbulence and weather. We were flying through a broken to overcast layer, and since it was dark, we couldn't determine the clouds ahead, but once in a while saw a few lights on the ground. It was not too long before the freezing level came down to us, or we climbed into it, and light ice started forming on the wing and props. At level off at the initial altitude of 8,000 feet, we set cruise power. Very carefully we set the manifold pressure to 31 inches of Mercury with the throttles and reduced the RPM of the engines to 2100 RPM using the propeller control. The co-pilot switches ON the AUTO LEAN light on the enunciator panel. The flight engineer located in the pylon or 'tower' under the wing set the fuel mixture controls of the engines to auto lean. The AUTO RICH MIXTURE light went out indicating the flight engineer had changed the fuel mixture from auto rich

to auto lean.. The flight engineer then moved the Carburetor Heat controls to move the Carburetor Air Temperature as close as possible to freezing and still not allow ice to form in the carburetor. Warm air prevents ice from forming in the carburetor, but too much reduces engine power resulting in a slower speed and reducing its range.

The pilots' throttles and propeller controls in the SA-10 cockpit were located in the ceiling instead of at the level of the control wheel; the more familiar location for land planes. The remaining engine controls are with the flight engineer in his position under the wing. The engineer controlled the mixture, carburetor heat, cowl flaps, fuel selectors and possessed a set of engine instruments. The pilot and co-pilot flight controls, two big control wheels, are connected by a brace between them containing a long rectangular enunciator panel. The panel was a type of signaling system harking back to naval ships. The panel contained lights co-located with small switches. The lights identify different items concerning the operation of the airplane controlled by the

flight engineer. For example, on this flight the RAISE FLOATS light would be lit until ready to land on the water. Other lights were either ON or OFF indicating the status of the items [Mixture settings, Stop Engines, Recall, etc]. The interphone could be used to request these items be activated or turned off; however it wasn't as handy as moving one switch. For example, In order to use the interphone to tell someone to do something, you first selected INTERCOM on the COMM box, then picked up a hand mike, pushed the mike button and talked.

The light, dry ice didn't pose an immediate problem, but over the long haul, it was going to eat into the fuel load. Even a small percentage of those 1275 gallons was a lot of fuel at the end of the flight. We kept very good records on the fuel flow, power settings and felt we could predict a problem well ahead of time. The fuel situation was pretty straightforward: the right tank feeds the right engine and the left tank feeds the left engine. Of course, there were provisions to feed fuel from a single tank to both engines, a feature we were to use towards the end of the flight. Since the temperature at altitude was just below freezing, some cabin heat had to be expended as well. We carried warm flight clothing, but some modification of the temperature was needed. The cabin heat took some of the high octane fuel as well, but it was a small amount. The SA-10 was not considered a sealed unit, and wind came through the body like a gentle breeze. Hardly any openings to the outside possessed a tight seal. We remember that the original PBY was really designed to fight in the Pacific; although they are used from the tropics to the Arctic with very little modification. Did we wear gloves? You betcha.

Cape Harrison radio, the Adcock Radio Range on the Labrador coast, was ahead and coming in strong. The Adcock Range was the old, repeat old, low frequency range designed for navigation that had four quadrants: two N [Morse code = dah dit] and two A quadrants [dit dah]; and when you were located on one of the four legs [the area in between the A and the N], the pilot would hear the two signals filling each other to produce a solid tone. Neat arrangement, but for some reason none of the courses were laid out from Goose to Cape Harrison. Fortunately, the radio frequency is covered by the automatic direction finder radios. The automatic direction finder did a good job in pointing us in the right direction. The signal was steady, allowing us to track our course over the ground. As we approached the coastline and Cape Harrison radio, the navigator picked up the non-directional beacon at Hopedale, Labrador on the other direction finder radio. Hopedale was about 75 miles north and our second checkpoint, so after a short discussion we cut the corner to fly direct towards Hopedale and save a few minutes.

The flight plan short cut at Cape Harrison Radio saved only a few miles, but it was important to save time and fuel. The flight plan was to proceed to Cape Harrison, then the short leg north to the fishing village of Hopedale. Past Hopedale, the course followed the Labrador coast north again to the northern tip of Labrador [no radio beacon there]. After the pointed tip of Labrador, we would fly over Resolution Island just to the north, then continuing to the non-directional beacon at Frobisher Bay, Baffin Island. Baffin Island is a huge island containing large stretches of land mass, mountains, and thousands of smaller islands.

Baffin Island 'complex' stretches from just north of Labrador to well above the Arctic Circle. From Frobisher Bay, it was important to establish a good position, and then track out of the beacon towards Padloping Island. The weather station at Padloping Island had no beacon for us to home on. They had and used the normal communications radio transmitters, but our automatic direction finders did not cover the frequency of these radio stations. In addition, navigation was complicated by the very big difference between True North and Magnetic North. The correction was not only large; it changed from 37 degrees West to 45 degrees West Variation between Goose Bay and Padloping Island.

Daylight arrived eventually, but most of the time we spent in the clouds, so the only change was being able to see the instrument panel easier. Occasionally, we could see the surface, but not often. The navigator could do a small amount of map reading to determine where we were. The small amount of ice and the drag it produced was a constant concern, and the subject of the infrequent interphone conversation. We could knock a little ice off the wings and tail surfaces with the de-icer boots, but we couldn't clean it all off, nor could we clean it from the big wing struts, radar or other surfaces. The small amount of ice increased drag, which reduced our indicated speed. We reduced power in cruise every hour or so, and there was always the question of skipping the power reduction to maintain a higher speed. The differences in numbers were small and we discussed this question more than once. Is it better to fly the published best indicated speed for that weight and altitude, or the published best power setting? As fuel burned off, the engine power and airspeed should be reduced to maintain the best angle of attack. My feeling was that the lowest drag was the best airspeed reference. The differences would be small, but we were going to be up there a long time.

The radio operator was kept busy getting out position reports and requesting weather information up the line. Most of the communications was the old fashion way: Morse code [dit dah dit]. His main contact was Goose Airways, a radio communications unit that relayed information to and from aircraft to air traffic control and weather stations, functioning much like the FAA Flight Service today. The radio communications were time consuming and occasionally the radio operator was required to manually re-tune the Collins radio to a new frequency. This is no mean task, taking sometimes ten minutes to retune and reset the radio. The radio operator's radio worked best with a long antenna, so the plane was equipped with a trailing wire antenna, which trailed from the bottom of the plane. A large streamlined lead weight on the end kept trailing straight. Occasionally, with a large frequency shift, the trailing wire would be moved in or out to provide the correct antenna length.

During the hours on the trip north the course was parallel along the Labrador northern coastline, so the young radar operator had plenty of practice in setting up and reading the radar. This was a World War II radar, an APS-3 with Yogi antennas mounted one on each wing, unlike the more modern dish antenna inside a radome. The yogi antenna on each wing looked much like the TV antennas in later years. It was pretty basic, but for land/water contrast it seemed to work. I went back a few times to see how he was doing and could see the problems. In my early days as an enlisted man, I was a radar repairman for a short period, and I felt I was qualified to interpret the radarscope. The land to the west is full of lakes – hundreds of them of various sizes and shapes, but the radar scope was clear enough to only pick out large and distinctive lakes. The result was a confusing picture that did little to refine our position. Labrador comes to a narrow section at the northernmost point, and this land/water contrast was apparent. The navigator was confident – and that was a good thing – and he was happy that we have only a small tail wind. A stronger tailwind would cost us much fuel on the return to Goose Bay while flying into the wind.

Navigation to Padloping Island up on the Baffin Island chain was very basic considering the equipment available today. The APN-7 LORAN worked fine, but our flight location was near an area called the

'LORAN baseline extension' where the fixes were unreliable. The navigator kept a good log of events, so the dead reckoning aspect would allow a good trail of where we had been. Celestial navigation was practical at that latitude, especially if you get on top; but a fix taken out of the wandering heading of the SA-10 took the phrase 'nav' out of navigation. The 'modern' addition of Visual Omni Range navigation had yet to make it to the Northeast in 1951, so the most accurate and useful navigation tool was the Automatic Direction Finding radio, or ADF. Unfortunately, there were few radio beacons along this flight path.

We were flying on an instrument flight clearance; however ironically we didn't have very good navigation aids to help us navigate in the clouds or on top. The good news was that there was no one else dumb enough to be out here and hence no traffic interference and zero chance of a collision with another plane. Except for the radio operator, there had been no radio communications by the pilots since leaving the Goose Bay control tower frequency.

Further north icing continued to be a small but nagging problem. Still there were numbing concerns about fuel consumption rather than an immediate need to get out of the ice. There was no easy way out, but it wasn't all that bad, since we continued to work the deicer boots and prop alcohol. The yogi antenna for the radar continued to collect ice as well. After the tip of Labrador, Resolution Island slid by on the right, and was spotted both on the ancient radar and visually. Much later, as we approached Frobisher Bay we checked for weather, winds and availability for fuel. The weather was just below the minimum altitude for a Non Directional Beacon approach. Checking the fuel remaining we found out we were still OK for the flight, and would be technically overweight for a water takeoff from Frobisher Bay. Adding more fuel weight would not be that dangerous, but we decided it was prudent to overfly Frobisher. I am sure the 'Frobishers,' a Canadian crew, were disappointed, since our arrival in that big flying boat would probably bump into and smash a few thousand mosquitoes. It was time for another power reduction.

Since we had three pilots on board, we changed seats now and then to give everyone a shot at the front of the plane. I felt the pressure of doing everything just right and probably spend a great deal more time in the cockpit than the other two – in fact, long enough for them to bring this to my attention. Still, I was the Pilot in Command and I wanted to be up front where I could see what was going on. Nervous energy kept me moving about the plane when I wasn't in one of the pilot seats, checking with the radar operator, the radio operator, navigator, flight engineer and the flight surgeon. As explained, the intercom was difficult to use and since it went to all positions on the plane at once, only one discussion at a time was practical.

The large area of water north of Frobisher Bay was Cumberland Sound, over a hundred miles wide. We could make out through the breaks in the clouds hundreds of islands and inlets on the north and south shores. By noontime, we were getting far enough north where some areas of Baffin Island on the map were printed in white [i.e. "no altitude information available"] scattered all over the chart.

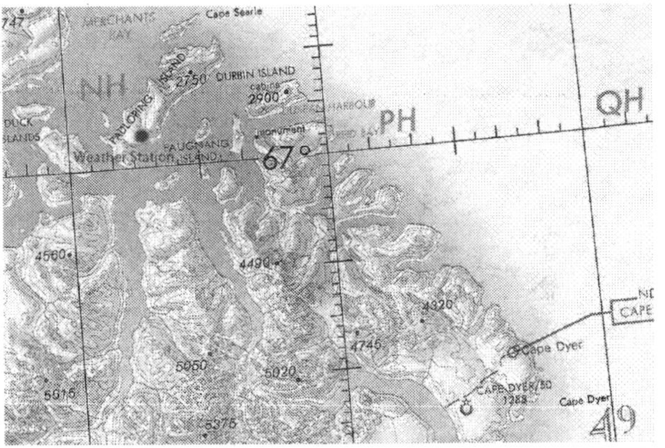

Unfortunately, we had to go over a few of these areas, so we started a second climb to get on top to at least protect ourselves as best possible. Eventually we did end up between cloud layers and we could see the mountains through breaks in the clouds. We remained between layers until the upper layer disappeared. Most mountains appeared higher than the estimates on the map. One such was marked "8,000 plus or minus" and looked much higher [looking at a more reliable map of today, the 8,000 was fairly close].The weather continued to get better and cloud deck below us broke up little by little as we proceeded north. It gave us pause to think about flying through that area on instruments, not knowing for sure the surface heights.

The last terrain on the trip was the rough mountains of the Cumberland Peninsula, a distance of two hundred miles of extremely inhospitable land. The area offered countless places to set down in case of trouble, although there did not appear to be any towns or villages anywhere in sight. As far as we could determine from the cockpit, there were areas untouched by human beings. Of course the Indians were old timers to this area, but we could not see any evidence of them.

Finally when Padloping Island appeared in front of us, the visibility allowed us to see the island clearly from 25 or 30 miles away. This was good news, since we didn't have to go searching for a hole to let down over the water, and then try to find the island. There was no navigation aid for approach at the island. Padloping Island looked like all the rest of the small chunks of land in the area, but it was well defined and was easily identified. Descent en route was made with low power to conserve fuel. Once down near the surface, we made a low pass over the weather station and then the landing area to check for debris and ice. We started the before landing preparations and the checklist between the pilots and the flight engineer. The copilot switches on the LOWER FLOATS light and soon the RAISE FLOATS light went out. The radio operator reported he was reeling in the trailing wire antenna. At the far end of the landing area, the outer bay was nearly covered with ice flows and the wind was blowing it towards the weather station. We set up our plane on the downwind leg and reviewed the checklist again. The landing was uneventful and we were led by a power boat to a large mooring buoy near the weather station. The mooring buoy was the one the ships used and was almost too big [and too hard] for us to use with this aluminum airplane. We managed to 'dock' the plane by very carefully and slowly getting downwind of the buoy. We gently contacted the bumper on the buoy and secured the plane. The flight engineer gladly volunteered to stay with the airplane and keep it away from the steel buoy. We promised to bring him something to eat, but he wasn't worried about that. We were all transported by boat into the 'base' and immediately fed.

We were also offered a tour of the facility. No, no! We were interested in getting out of there before the ice got too close. They didn't get visitors very often and were looking forward to news from civilization other than the limited information they got over the Teletype every day. Their daily newspaper was the bulletin board, covered with the latest Teletype news. We finished our meal of roast beef sandwiches, soup and coffee and declared we would like to get going. We did get a quick look at the facility. The compound was one great big building made by connecting all the small buildings with tunnel-like passageways. The galley crew made a box lunch for the flight engineer, which we carried back to him.

The patient, an Air Force Captain, was ready to go - very nervous about the possibility of staying there until the Spring supply ship, but not overly thrilled with the prospect of going home in this aluminum boat. The Flight Surgeon checked him over and said he was OK to fly without any medication or use of the stretcher. The power boat transferred our crew to the plane a few at a time. Once at the mooring dock we got everyone briefed and ready to go, pushed off from the buoy. The aircraft slowly drifted back from the buoy, and we used the wind on the huge flight controls to turn the plane so that we were not pointed at the buoy. The flight engineer reported well over half the fuel load was remaining. Still no problem, but we couldn't waste any. We estimated that we had enough fuel for the return trip and have one hour of fuel remaining for a fuel reserve. Soon we were far enough from the buoy to safely start the engines, as the plane starts moving as soon as the first engine starts.

The engines started without a hesitation and we taxied away like we knew what we were doing. A quick engine run up [ah, that is a thrill, doing a magneto check on the water - - no brakes !] One last look down the inner bay and we started the takeoff. The SA-10 doesn't take long to get into the air, since the flying speed is quite low, but it seemed longer that day. The initial takeoff run is very nose high to get the plane riding on top of the water and visibility forward was severely limited, until the plane reached the point where it was on the 'step' and the nose lowered to a flatter attitude. Crisply airborne with the ice flow safely ahead, we picked up a heading back for Frobisher Bay, climbing to get back to a safe altitude. By this time it was mid to late afternoon. John turned on the RAISE FLOATS sign and a few seconds later the LOWER FLOATS light went out.

Initially, the return flight was more of the same, fairly good weather in the beginning and getting more cloud cover as we proceeded south. We planned to fly at a lower altitude once we were in the area of Resolution Island. The southern part of Cumberland Peninsula and Baffin Island slid under the airplane, unseen in the dusk. The crew settled down for the long trip back and more than one went by the patient to make him feel comfortable and at home. By the time we arrived over Frobisher Bay, it was dark and a landing there for fuel would be hazardous due to the cloud ceiling and lack of lighting for the seaway. We had enough fuel with a small reserve, so we droned on. Ahead lie Resolution Island and lastly the coastline of Labrador, so our radar guy could verify our position. We started a slow descent to 6,000 feet, hoping that headwinds would be less. The navigator was satisfied we were doing well, although the ground speed had slowed somewhat as expected. We were doing OK and still believed we had an hours fuel reserve. The night was black, without a moon. Once in a while we could see land or lake shapes below. We were still six and a half to seven hours from landing. Time to re-adjust the power setting, and maybe look into the in-flight lunch for a snack.

The final run down the coastline of Labrador was fairly uncomfortable. The radar operator was keeping us on track and allowing the navigator to get a fix now and then using the old radar set. *As I found out, the radarscope could verify where you were if you already knew where you were, but not that great when you didn't know where you were.* However, the continual worry over the ground speed caused much discussion about fuel reserve. The ground speed continued to fall off, a precursor to problems later on. The low ground speed was a worry, and somewhere North of the Cape Harrison radio we requested an intercept from the local Air Rescue

Squadron. We knew that we would be getting into Goose Bay during the night hours, and we did not have enough gas to last until daylight for a water landing. The radio operator was having increasing problems with radio contact with Goose Bay Airways.

Probably around midnight we could make out the Adcock Range signal a long ways ahead at Cape Harrison. The signal was identified by the Bendix radio, the HI-FI of the two radios. Turning the loop with a hand crank wasn't too much work when you are flying towards or away from a radio station, but it was a lulu on an instrument check. The Bendix worked great and we were confident we had the Cape Harrison radio locked on many miles north. We were concerned that the low ground speed was going to translate into low fuel and we wanted no mistakes in navigation. We needed to get to Goose Bay without wandering from course. Checking my watch, it showed I had been awake [excluding the cat naps at Goose] around 36 hours. We re-adjusted the engine power once more to save fuel.

We continued to grind on towards Cape Harrison radio and finally, the other ADF picked up the signal automatically giving a heading to the station. Life was good, two sets showing the same thing – basically on course like the navigator wanted – but a little slow. Finally, the Cape Harrison Adcock range station was getting close and we flew right over the station, going from the N-sector to an A sector and back to an N again. Station passage showed when the ADF bearing pointer swung around from the nose to the tail. We turned the plane for a heading to Goose Bay, and retuned the radios to the Goose frequencies.

Goose Bay was 125 NM away and normally the low frequency radio could be heard. Not this time. The navigator rechecked and confirmed the heading was correct. Not too many minutes later we tried to retune to the Cape Harrison radio on the Bendix. No joy. The set was silent except for the ever-present static. Through a break in the clouds we saw the lights of a small fishing village slip by. Little did we know that we would have welcomed the sight of them again later in the flight. We started a slow descent to four thousand to stay under the lowest cloud deck.

Where was that Rescue plane? They should have been airborne in 30 – 45 minutes, certainly by the time we reached Cape Harrison radio. The Goose Airways communications station advised their SB-17 was in the process of launching. Our radio operator is saying with his Morse code: Airways, what is our bearing from you? "Give me a ten-second tone" was the Morse code response. The tone went out, but they couldn't give us a bearing, and hence no vector for Goose Bay. The radio operator became concerned and kept requesting bearings in between other communications. Still no bearings were offered by the ground station, saying they were unable to give a bearing. By this time, it was obvious that we had flown into a radio 'black-out' area. This wasn't that uncommon up north, but usually there was a warning in advance.

Clearly, 30 minutes after passing Cape Harrison radio, we should have been able to talk to the control tower, seen the airport beacon and lights of Goose Bay. Finally, the estimated time of arrival for Goose Bay arrived and still no lights of the airport, no radio contact on the VHF frequencies with Goose Tower, and nothing on the great Bendix ADF radio. The navigator suggested trying the teletype frequency from Thule, Greenland, a powerful radio that he had used from time to time. Strangely, this radio came in fairly strong and the radio compass showed a fairly solid reading. Thule was 1500 or so miles away and a line of position off that radio was not useful. For some reason we could not find the teletype frequency at Goose Bay. These things weren't published as navigation aids. At this time, discussions between the pilots and the flight engineer centered on remaining fuel. We started the procedure for being lost, called the SQUARE SEARCH, expanding outward in all directions by making ever larger ground tracks around the last known position, and hoping for the Air Rescue SB-17 to check in with us.

"I have an idea Lieutenant," the engineer said, "I will even the fuel readings so both tanks are equal, then switch the engines to one tank, and we can measure the time it takes to run out of fuel." The idea was a great idea, actually, one of the best ideas in the last hour. So, the engineer leveled the fuel in the two tanks until the two readings were equal. After advising us the tanks held the same amount of fuel, we noted the time and switched fuel selectors to run both engines from the same tank.

In the meantime, the radio operator was working hard to get that bearing, the radar operator was trying to make sense of the mess on the scope. A large lake exists near Goose Bay by the name Lake Melville that should have been south of our track, but he couldn't find anything that met the description. The place was full of lakes and hills. We were lower now and the difficulty in reading the scope was increased. The radar scope would present the area behind a hill as a void, and appear the same as a lake. The navigator was trying different radio aids that he knew about – teletype transmitters that are very strong. Repeated calls went out to the Tower and the Rescue airplane but no response – almost as if the radios had failed. Intercom conversation was difficult, in that each transmission was to the full crew, which is good in one respect, but difficult for two teams of people to talk over two problems. Yes, and the discussions were also available to the passenger and Flight Surgeon, if they had a headset. Of course it was pitch black with no moon showing, the time was about two AM and we remained below an overcast layer. We expected to see the ground features, but everything was black. Our cockpit lights were already on minimum to allow us to see the ground. For some time we had been using the radio altimeter, a radar type instrument that bounced pulses vertically and the instrument on the panel showed the altitude above the ground.

Shortly, the fuel flow indicators at the flight engineer's station started fluctuating as the engines started to suck bits of air. Quickly, the engineer switched both engines to the other tank, and we checked the watches – 45 minutes had gone by. Now we knew when we had to be on the ground. A quick check of the fuel log indicated that the information was about right – our record keeping had been well above average. That was little satisfaction now. John Donahoe was in the right seat and decided to open the side window in an effort to see more.

About this time, the Rescue SB-17 checked in on VHF, calling us in the blind. I wanted to say, "Hey!! We're over here!!" but we quickly requested a steer or bearing. "Give me a 30 second tone" was the command from the 17, and we complied by holding down the mike button and pressing the TONE button on the VHF set. Silence on the other end. Finally the guy on the radio says, "Give me another 30 second tone." We gave them a second tone for them to locate our direction. The method and the homing device they were using required the pilot to turn the plane until the on-course signal was heard, very much like the on-course procedure for the Adcock range, except the letters were U and D [dit dit dah and dah dit dit]. Apparently, he was having trouble with the U-D homer. We transmitted, "If you are having problems, give us a 45 second tone, we have a homer too." Without hesitation the tone appeared and we turned on the homer and started the turn. A U signal [dit dit dah] would mean a right turn to find the solid tone – i.e. U turn right. I made a complete 360 without much change in the tone quality, no solid on course signal and a very weak and unclear U or D signal. We did notice a difference in signal level on two headings and passed this on to the Rescue SB-17. They agreed, telling us they had little or no change in the signal. The fuel was getting low, ... that is to say, VERY LOW.

Presently, John yelled out "There is a lake down there!" He took control and turned the plane to get a better look. I barely could make out what he was seeing. I took the plane back and turned to put the lake on my side. I slid back my window and could make out a difference in the shade of black below us. We set up a pattern around the lake to take a good look at it. Earlier we had been talking about bailing out using the parachutes we carried. I thought we should bail out the crew, figuring that someone would make it, rather than all of us going down in the plane. John and the other pilot, Jim Huffman, disagreed and talked me out of it. Now that we had an actual lake, the decision was easier. Huffman in the rear said, "I'll get those flares back here ready and we can make a landing under the flares – it would be a piece of cake." The engineer agreed, so they dug out the flares, got them ready to throw over the side and we readied everyone for the 'ditching.' Huffman later confirmed there were five flares. We discussed it, and decided that three were necessary for the landing. They only burn three minutes, someone reminded us. In the meantime, Donahoe in the right seat kept a running conversation with the Rescue SB-17 to try to locate our position.

It turned out the lake was quite small, but it was the only one we could see. The small size made it important to get it down at the beginning of the lake or end up in the trees at the far end. We had no idea of the wind on the surface – no weather reports out of Goose to go by, and we had no actual knowledge of the lake level – whether at sea level or a thousand feet. The lake was oriented East – West and I mentioned something about Greeley saying to 'Go West Young man' so we set up to land to the West [and after all, the prevailing wind is from the west, so the odds were with us]. The parachute flares were standard issue flares that burned for 3 minutes and descended about 1000 feet in that time. We started the landing checklist. FLOATS DOWN light goes on, and a second later we could hear the float actuating motors moving the floats to the extended position. FLOATS UP light goes out. Everyone was wearing a Mae West and was seated in their seats. The passengers were in the mid-section.

The flight engineer told us: "To save fuel, I will keep the mixtures in lean until you have to make a go around." Good thinking, but there is not enough fuel to go anywhere else, and not enough flares to light the surface for a second attempt. I liked his positive attitude though. Finally, the checklist was complete and we headed back over the lake.

We flew over the lake heading west, dropped a flare at the far end, made a left turn onto the downwind leg, and dropped a second flare. With landing lights on and power reduced, I started a descent on the downwind to get as low as I dared. The downwind seemed to take forever. The radio altimeter was moving frantically up and down as it measured the terrain under us. I could barely make out the approach end of the lake from the downwind leg.

Turning base, we dropped the final flare, I pulled throttles all the way back, and started as steep a descent as I dared. The first flare was now ahead of us and we could see we were lined up with the lake. As we rolled wings level on final approach, the flare ahead burned out or failed. Looking up towards the second flare to the left, there was NO flare [it had hit the ground on a hill beside the lake]. The flare behind us was burning bright WHITE; but DID NOT ILLUMINATE the area straight ahead of us. Trying to find something in the landing lights, I could see the trees on the lake shore as we passed over. How high were we? Hold this attitude – power off and nose low. I glanced over my left shoulder at the flare behind us. It was still burning brightly and all of the terrain was brilliantly lighted! [What an urge to do a quick 180 degree turn! I fought the urge.] I made a judgment of height looking over my shoulder and started to bring the nose up to ease the descent. The landing lights showed nothing now, so there was water below us.

BLAM! The plane hit the water and bounced. As the artificial horizon reached a positive nose-up attitude, I tried to hold that attitude with elevator control and the plane hit again; blam, not so hard this time. Again we ballooned into the air, but this time the nose got high enough for us for an easy nose-high touchdown. The plane plowed to a slow speed – still nothing showing in the landing lights.

"WE'RE SINKING.!! WE'RE SINKING !!" was the frantic call from in back of the plane.

The engineer dropped down from his perch in the tower and called out, "We're taking on some water, but it's OK Lieutenant. Get it on a beach!"

I believed I saw a shoreline to the right in the reflection of the landing lights, but when I added power to the left engine the plane simply did not want to turn right. In the dim reflection of the lights the shoreline appeared to have a low vertical wall – not so good for beaching, so I added power to the right engine and turned promptly left 90 degrees left to look for a beach. It didn't take long, since the lake was small and narrow, and the landing lights started picking up details as we got closer to the shoreline. The 'beach' was littered with big rocks, but we were headed into an area clear of visible rocks and proceeded to taxi slowly until the bottom of the plane started touching the bottom. The sound of the plane on the bottom was the soft hiss of sliding over sand or mud. We added power to keep moving.

We wanted to get the plane close to shore and in shallower water. Finally, the plane wouldn't move any further and we were fairly high and dry. It looked like the nose was only 5 or 10 feet from the shoreline. Shining a flashlight down behind me in the crew compartment, I could see the water coming in from the nose wheel compartment. It was not a torrent, but definitely coming in. We found out later that the first impact and possibly the second impact were on the nose wheel doors and the impact shattered the plastic water seals between the nose wheel compartment and the crew compartment. Once on the water, we could confirm the wind was very light, with no waves to show speed or direction.

Once we were stopped and had a chance to get our thoughts together and check to see if everyone was OK, we lowered the landing gear to keep the plane from moving. There was one injury. Lieut. Jim Huffman was in the blister or gunners area in the rear to drop the flares and was watching the landing while still standing at the position. He was knocked off his feet and broke his nose. Not too bad, considering that we all could have been dead by now. Most of the crew set about to get out of the plane and onto shore to find out what the conditions were. The crew broke out the survival kit and started an inventory.

In the final portion of the landing, we were still broadcasting tones to the Rescue plane. Eventually they could reach us on VHF while we were on the water. Soon they flew over the lake with a big show of landing lights. In one of the brief conversations we had, we tried to find out where we were. The answer came back in some sort of left handed English leaving us with the idea that we were South of Goose Bay. That didn't bother us. They could have said we were outside of Detroit and we had no argument to disprove it. The truth was that we were North of Goose Bay, but we wouldn't know that until later in the day. Final count, everyone on board was safe, and the only injury was the broken nose of Huffman's. The 'patient' was shaken but OK and the Flight Surgeon was just glad to be alive.

The crew started setting up camp in the meantime, so we set out to find what was in the survival kit and the stores on the plane. A couple of hours later when daylight showed our position, we could see that the airplane was parked in the only stretch without large boulders. It was blind luck, but we hit that one part of the beach….somebody guided us in?

The wooded area was very close to the water, so the term beach is more symbolic than descriptive. We settled on a narrow stretch of reasonably smooth surface and started to set up shelters. A couple of the fellows walked further down the beach in the direction of landing and reported back that the lake on the other side of a small piece of land was a couple of miles long [more like five as it turned out]; but we never did see the larger lake while in the air. In the meantime, the nose wheel door seals continued to leak until the water level inside the plane reached the level of the lake. So, we are stuck on the beach, but the people were looking into the survival kit with relish.

Early morning, a Canadian Air Force [RCAF] single-engine Norseman airplane on floats landed on the lake to pick up our patient and the Flight Surgeon. Huffman had a broken nose and he went with them. The Norseman also brought fuel in the floats as well. We dutifully pumped it into the SA-10, but we felt the plane was going to be here for a long, long time. The pilot also explained where we were, which was a great deal different than the understanding a few hours before, but again, we had no information to say it was wrong. The pilot of the plane also said work was afoot to come in and get us with another SA-10. The Norseman left, and we went back to surviving.

You probably won't have any difficulty believing that the near disaster left us a little giddy. The relief after several hours of believing you were soon dead, leaves you with the feeling that everything else is funny. After several lively discussions about our situation and what to do with it, we concluded that we really did need to get to know that rifle in the kit – you never know when a bear might come out of the woods. The rifle was a 22 caliber/410 gauge over-under. There was a small supply of ammo. We decided to calibrate the rifle by shooting at a certain rock out in the lake. The rifle was pretty good, and we managed to hit the rock several times, until someone discovered that the remaining ammo wasn't sufficient to fight off a bear. We shut down the rifle range. The most trouble came when the airplane returned home a week later and we had to explain the loss of the rifle ammo. In the Air Force, losing the ammo was nearly on the level of murder and treason.

Back at the home base at Ernest Harmon AFB, they had been busy putting together a maintenance team to recover the SA-10. Our unit cranked up the other amphibian and early afternoon the SA-10 showed up and landed on the lake next door. The pilot said he would have been crazy to land in the same lake we used. The maintenance people inspected the damage, finding only a slightly dented door and the rear seals broken. They could rotate the plane slightly by retracting the landing gear, then retracting the floats and keeping one float in the water. They decided what they needed to bring back when they brought the recovery team. We slept on the replacement SA-10 that night. I was allowed to use one of the bunks, which gave me the first real sleep in fifty some hours.

The next morning, we gathered everything together, tied the wounded SA-10 securely to the shore, and left two men to stay and guard the plane. These people, the Land Rescue Team, had arrived with the airplane and would enjoy the camping out, and setting up the camp for the repair crew. After all that was accomplished, we roared off the 'long' lake and flew back to Ernest Harmon and our families. Due to the poor [i.e. slow] communications in those days, the people back at Harmon knew very little for the first half day of the excitement. The word went out initially that we were 'down' in Labrador someplace. Later they found out we were alive, but little else. So, we celebrated at the club that night for a long time, telling wild tales of the night over Labrador.

The next day, the squadron launched the recovery crew in the SA-10 that brought us home. I felt I should go back with them and bring it out, since I was the one that put it in there. But the maintenance officer was qualified in the SA-10 and he had to be there anyway. Up to that point, a determination had not been made whether the landing and resultant damage was an incident or an accident, or what type accident. That was finally made, following the return of the SA-10 to the home base.

The recovery of the SA-10 was a tale that deserves more detail than I can provide. The recovery crew involved the maintenance people and supervisor [actually three or four people], some land rescue specialists to run and maintain the camp and prepare the meals. The mechanics performed a remarkable job in replacing one of the nose wheel doors and the seals between the nose wheel compartment and the crew compartment. Wearing survival suits, they worked crouching in the cold water with their heads above water and hands underneath. They did the necessary wrench work by feel. The seals were repaired from inside the plane, but still knee deep in water.

Finally, the work was done, the water pumped out, and the plane 'sort of' re-floated. It floated in the channel we dug as we were driving it up to the beach. The night the job was finished, the whole crew celebrated with a big turkey dinner from the military C-Rations and what little else the survival specialists brought. They had some beer, turkey, soup and what they said was all the trimmings. During the evening the main discussion was how to turn the SA-10 to head out from the beach, since the plane did not have reverse pitch on the propellers. Very little force could be applied to pull it from the beach. They tried to set an anchor a hundred feet behind the plane and pull it off by pulling on the cable, but without success. Idea after idea was brought up and discussed amid the ample flow of beer, but they could not reach an agreement on a well thought out plan. "Let's think about it and look at it again in the morning."

That night a storm brewed up with wind and rain battering their tents and howling through the trees. By this time they were all in the tents with the lamps out and were not aware of the effect of the wind on the plane. The SA-10 had been secured by strong ropes between the nose tie down and the trees on the shoreline and nothing was going to break it loose. HOWEVER, when they awoke the next morning and got to the plane to check for damage, they found the plane parked still on the beach, but sitting parallel to the beach! The strong wind blowing during the night, was blowing so that it turned the plane slowly in the tie down ropes. The old SA-10 was ready to taxi out ! All they had to do was make a right turn and head for deeper water. After breaking camp and packing away the equipment and tools, the two crews departed their respective lakes. The pilot flying out of the short lake accelerated downwind and made a running turn into the wind at the end of the lake, this gave him the momentum to accelerate to takeoff speed without a problem. Light on fuel, it headed for Goose Bay for some high octane, then home to Harmon.

Back at Harmon the plane could be inspected for damage and to determine if it had been an accident and if so, what level of accident. After much discussion, it was determined that the event was a minor accident, and the safety officer started his investigation in earnest. We had already made statements and told our story to the squadron commander, but there are always forms to fill out.

The accident report went forward to the Group Commander, located in St. Johns, Newfoundland, citing the circumstances of radio blackout preventing proper navigation and/or the bearings from the Airways Station. He forwarded the report to the Air Rescue Service Headquarters, where they would analyze and file the report.

Along with the accident report, the squadron commander forwarded a separate commendation for the Air Medal for me. He was so glad to get his airplane and crew back in one piece, he felt the successful blackout landing deserved the recognition. He cited the achievement of the successful landing despite extenuating circumstances of the mission, the lack of outside aid. The Group commander endorsed the recommendation to Air Rescue Headquarters for their consideration and approval.

Weeks passed and presently, the accident report was sent back through channels to the Group Commander for more information. They felt they needed additional information about the weather, radio blackout information and other details. It was necessary to go to Goose Bay to retrieve this information, and as it happened, I was scheduled to go to Goose Bay to provide rescue coverage of one of the jet fighter crossings of the Atlantic.

The safety officer and the commander gave me a list of things to find out while I was on the ground at Goose Bay. The idea of me investigating my own accident wasn't considered any breach, since I was innocent and a probable recipient of the Air Medal. Besides they didn't have a cheap way to get someone else to Goose Bay.

Arrival at Goose Bay had its moments of terror and hilarity. On this flight I was flying a C-82, the original FLYING BOX CAR, transporting a helicopter through there to Greenland. After landing and securing the aircraft, an irate full colonel roared up to the airplane in a jeep. He jumped out and came up to me nose to nose.

"What are you doing here at Goose Bay?" was the shouted question over the noise on the ramp. I answered back that I was there to refuel and RON.

"This air base is closed to transient traffic! You aren't supposed to be here!" was the loud and irritated reply.

I told him, "I didn't see anything in the NOTAMs."

"NOTAMs, Hell, it is Secret!" he yelled back.

I explained that I was on my way to BW1 [Narrassark Air Field] in Greenland. I was to leave the next day for a rescue support mission for some jet fighters. That quieted him down since apparently that was the classified movement he was talking about. He left in the jeep just before we started laughing.

I had a few details to work out on the accident investigation before going to the club and Visiting Officers Quarters. First stop was the Base Operations Officer. I explained what I was doing and what records I needed [clearance, weight and balance, etc] and then on to the Weather Station. Again I told him of my purpose and requested the weather charts for the time before, during and after the accident. The Base Ops driver drove me over to the Airways Station administrative office, and I went through the explanation again, asking for the logs for the station on certain frequencies for the times needed. This done, I headed for the club to see some friends. I would pick up the information when I came back from Greenland. All is well as the accident investigation team members belly up to the bar.

The Greenland mission was concluded without any problems since the jets all got to Iceland without losing anyone.

On the return to Goose Bay, I went to the Base Operations, weather and the Airways people and retrieved my records. I read them carefully to make sure they gave me the proper information. It looked

OK; however I noticed that during the two or two and one-half hours we were trying to get a Direction Finding bearing out of the Airways people, there actually were three bearings logged in the communications log. The note explained they were CLASS C and couldn't be passed on to the aircraft. The radio blackout had deteriorated the radio signals to the point where the signal strength was low and contained interference. As it turned out, the bearings were reasonable considering the times and where we ended up. We would later tie these times in with the navigation log to see if they would have helped. It looked to me that we would have at least taken a heading towards Goose Bay.

Back at Harmon, I turned in the information to the safety officer and commander with a special note of the attempt to get a bearing out of the Airways guys and them actually getting bearings, but not passing them on. They jumped on that with both feet. The safety officer went over all of the material and pointed out that the weather maps before and after the accident showed a deep low formed during our flight.

"Jones, you had a 50 – 55 knot crosswind after leaving Cape Harrison Radio!" and continued, "You would have a 25 – 30 degree drift in that P-Boat." The safety officer again assembled the accident report in a new endorsement to the report including the new information. The endorsement was sent to the Group commander for his further endorsement to Headquarters Air Rescue.

Again weeks passed and one day a message arrived asking for the commander and myself and any other crewmembers from that flight to report to the Group headquarters. The next day we took an airplane to the Torbay airport near St. Johns. The Group Commander, a very nice guy, explained that the most recent endorsement to the report came back asking for more detailed information. He stated that it looked like the headquarters Air Rescue Service was going to find somebody to blame and he didn't feel it should be him. Because of the pressure to find a culprit, he reassessed the accident findings. He elected to change the findings from: 80% - Act of God [weather and radio blackout] and 20%

Airways Communications. The Group commander decided the accident causes should be: Act of God [weather & blackout]- 40%, Airways – 20%, Pilot error – 25%, and Navigator error – 15%.The reason for the pilot error was not specified, but probably for dinging the nose wheel door. The navigator was given his error for his 'attempt' to tune in an unauthorized radio aid and for not insisting on climbing on top to take a celestial fix. Of course, we did nothing with the useless information from the Thule teletype and the navigator would have had an argument trying to convince us to climb up on top when we were so short of fuel. The celestial fix – a three line triangle would probably have been bigger than the state of Michigan had we completed it. Oh well, it was a tough call to breakout percentages, but the 40% crew error equaled the largest other factor. I give him this much. He called me over there to tell me to my face.

Several weeks later, a letter was endorsed back to the squadron, through the Group, from Hq, Air Rescue. The letter to the Group commander referenced the commendation for the Air Medal for a Lieut. Jones and the 9th endorsement to the accident report that assigned 25% pilot error to Lieut. Jones. What was his recommendation for the Air Medal? The Group commander replied that the commendation was being withdrawn. So there it was: The Air Medal downgraded to twenty-five per cent pilot error.

THE NEWFOUNDLAND FISHING CAMP

When I was a young Lieut. in Newfoundland, one of the aircraft I flew was a PBY flying boat. We called it the SA-10, or between us PBY pilots, the PigBoat. One day we were to escort a C-82 cargo airplane. The C-82 had the job of dropping two aircraft floats out of the back

File photo

door, into a lake for the base people [and visiting Colonels] to use for fishing and hunting. The Air Force had a campsite at one of the many lakes and we used to take people in and pick them up.

Since releasing an airplane float out of the cargo hold had never been done, they thought it prudent to send a seaplane that could land and pick up the pieces if 'something' happened. The C-82 released the first float [and the parachute pack], but the airflow forced the float up into the elevator damaging it, before falling into the lake below. The crew of the 'Packet' as it was called, decided the best thing to do was to go home since the law of averages said the second float was going to complete the job. They headed home, and I followed.

Because of the damage they flew slow. I saw my opportunity to show them what a PBY looked like passing them [something that would as rare as a virgin birth]. The PBY was not speedy, maybe 110 knots on a clear day, so I slowly climbed up behind him and off to one side, and leaving full power on, started a descent to catch up and pass him. It worked so good, I decided to feather the propeller on his side. We slipped past him with the one propeller standing still and as the speed fell off we turned away to get behind them again. They were serious about their problem and didn't see any humor in the joke.

They returned to Harmon Air Base and landed without incident. Of course that left the remaining aircraft float at the base, with the delivered one useless as a platform. As the Rescue Squadron had suggested in the first place, the second float was delivered by PBY. During WWII, the PBY used to carry torpedoes under the wing to deliver torpedoes to submarines. The mechanism was still installed and worked fine using some padding device between the float and the plane. Thus it happened, the two floats were connected between two flat sheets of wood to form a floating platform. It worked fine at the campsite to move around the lake, outboard motor and all.

The rescue squadron's C-82 was used at the lake on at least one occasion.

The rescue squadron flew several different types of planes, depending on the need, and most pilots were checked out in two or more types. This story fits in with the story of the lake and the recreation uses it provided.

One day, I was asked to take the C-82 and air-drop some supplies into a camp of men on a moose hunting trip. I don't remember why they needed additional food and stuff, usually they went well equipped. Every package was fitted with a small cargo chute and we launched to go to the lake in the southeastern part of Newfoundland. These people were taken in by PBY and probably should have been re-supplied by PBY, but as always, it wasn't my choice to ask why, only 'when do I leave?'.

We found the camp location quickly, but no one was at the camp to signal us where to drop the supplies. Ah-h-h there they are over in that marshy area! We flew down low to attract their attention, hoping for someone to let us know where to start dropping the packages. They didn't like that, and instead of waving, they appeared to be shaking their fists! As I found out later, they were stalking a moose and we caused the moose to run away. They didn't forget this for many months. We swung by the campsite again, and someone finally was showing a flag to attract us. He had moved to a life raft and rowed off shore a short ways, easily marking the camp as the target. He couldn't tell us what he wanted on the radio, and was actually waving the white flag back and forth in what he perceived as a negative or NO signal. We proceeded to start dropping the packages, four as I remember, one per low pass.

As the Colonel explained a week later when we were chewed out for chasing the moose and continuing the air drop, they changed their mind about needing supplies. In the excitement of trying to find a card in his wallet that explained hand signals, he dropped his wallet in the lake, and it sank with all of his ID cards and X dollars in cash. He made the suggestion that the aircrew reimburse him for the cash, but the Base Commander nixed that idea.

Bringing a moose out of the camp back to Ernest Harmon AFB was always a tough job. I had the privilege only once. The work of loading onto the PBY was done one-quarter or so at a time. Placing a quarter in a life raft and the PBY floating in the lake. The job of lifting a moose quarter involved people in the airplane and in the life raft. The raft did not have a firm bottom so as the people attempted to lift the moose, their feet sunk into the plastic floor. As a result, the majority of work was done by the people leaning over the edge of the rear hatch, or blister as it was called. Repeat this until you had a whole moose in the plane. Once in the aircraft, the moose was moved forward to the main compartment. Did blood get in the interior? You betcha. A later job for the aircraft ground crew to clean and sterilize. After loading the complete moose, the rest of the transportation was easy. The PBY handled the added weight without so much as a shrug and unloading back at the base sitting on the cement was a piece of cake compared to the job back at the lake.

Sometimes you want to refer to those times as the "The Good Old Days."

FLYING THE C-82 AT MONCTON, NOVA SCOTIA

"Lt. Jones, Major Emmons wants you up on the flight deck," came the call from the ladder that allowed access from the cargo bay some 9 or 10 feet up to the flight deck. I hustled up the ladder to find out what Major Emmons wanted. I had a clue, since we were all aware of an oil leak from the left engine.

"What can I do for you Major?" I yelled to Major Emmons through the engine noise. Emmons was sitting in the pilot seat on the left side of the huge cockpit.

"Get in the right seat Don, we need your help," he called out and as I put on the headset he explained to me about the oil leak on the left engine and how the oil was getting in or close to the heat exchanger that was soaking up engine exhaust heat and was nearly red hot. The engineer and also crew chief cut in with, "I think we ought to shut the engine down and feather the prop before we have a fire. There is no way to put the fire out in that area." Emmons added, "You are an instructor pilot in the C-82 and I want your agreement to do this," to which I replied let's get started and picked up the checklist.

How did I get in this position, from being a passenger on the plane to being the instructor pilot and probably going to share in any fault-finding that will occur later? Well, it started out like most tales ". . . there I was . . . ,"

The squadron was in the process of converting from the amphibian search plane, the SA-10 to the new Grumman SA-16. We ferried two of the SA-10/PBYs from the home base in Stephenville, Newfoundland to a depot at Mobile, Alabama. I was the pilot in one of the planes. It was a slow and long flight, but both planes made the trip without mishap or any adventure worth mentioning. As commercial travel was expensive, it was the custom to use another plane in the squadron to pick up the six crewmembers and fly them back to Newfoundland.

This was good flying time, and the unit had one Fairchild C-82, and it was chosen to make the trip. The squadron Operations Officer, Major Perry Emmons selected himself as the pilot and picked two other pilots to go and share the flying. Neither of these pilots was current in the C-82 and this was a good opportunity to get some experience. They made the trip to Mobile, Alabama and were ready to return us to Newfoundland.

The flight back was routine and we landed at Westover AFB for an overnight stay and fuel. The crew chief found a problem that required a cylinder change on the left R-2800 engine. The cylinder did not develop enough power and a weakened and rough engine resulted. The engineer/crew chief with the assistance of the SA-10/PBY flight engineers and some mechanics at Westover did change the cylinder in record time. The next morning after a thorough run-up, we departed Westover with the six passengers and four crewmembers for a routine trip to Harmon AF Base at Stephenville. The weather looked pretty good, the crew got the plane on top of the clouds and 'us passengers' found a place to rest our bones in the canvas troop seats that was the sum of all the passenger conveniences. We certainly didn't take up much room in that cavern that was called the cargo compartment. The C-82 called the 'Packet,' was famous for having the inside cargo dimensions of a freight car! We could have held a bowling tournament in the place. The cargo hold was not noted for a warm place to be, and the engine noise was very loud. A few hours in the cargo area, you felt the vibration deep inside your bone marrow. Sleep? No way, the only hope was the sound vibrations would beat you senseless and you would drift off to oblivion.

The flight continued on peacefully on top of the clouds with little or no turbulence. Except for the sound of the propellers pounding in the head, it was going well. One of the PBY/SA-10 crew chiefs was up looking around outside and reported a small oil leak on the left engine. He pointed it out to the flight engineer of the C-82 and he maintained a frequent watch on the leak.

Now an oil leak was not the end of the world in these old round engines and the eighteen cylinder R-2800 had plenty of opportunities built in to produce a leak. A small oil leak was hunted down and repaired when time permitted, but it didn't normally affect a particular flight. The joke was that the leak shouldn't be so bad that you ran out of oil before getting on the ground, A small amount of oil spread by the slipstream would look like a lot more oil than was actually coming out. I was blissfully unaware of the goings on about the oil leak. I was 'slunk down' in the canvas seat trying to get a nap while the cymbal sounds of the engines and props beat into my ears.

Finally, when the call came from the flight deck to come up, I was quickly brought up to speed. For one, I didn't know where we were, and only had a vague notion of the length of time we had been in the air.

By the time we got the left engine shut down and the propeller feathered to stop the rotation of the engine, enough oil had entered the heat exchanger to start a stream of dark smoke. I asked where we were, and Perry gave me a quick briefing. We were south of Moncton, Nova Scotia where we would pick up the outbound heading towards Stephenville, Newfoundland and Harmon AF Base. We had about an hour to go to reach Harmon on that one engine. I asked about the amount of fuel aboard, and the engineer believed we had enough, but we were using a large amount of fuel with the high engine power.

The plane was barely holding altitude with the power at essentially full power, and at a very slow airspeed, which was expected. We were at 8,000 feet and the Packet wasn't known for its single engine high altitude performance. We got permission to descend to a lower altitude and this improved the airspeed problem for a few minutes.

We had a serious discussion about continuing the flight on one engine. If we ran into trouble with the other engine, the flight engineer said he didn't want to start up that left engine again. After a few minutes, we decided that it was not prudent to continue to Harmon. The weather at Moncton was reported to be at the minimums for the Automatic Direction Finding approach that was their mainstay. Just short of Moncton beacon we explained the problem to the Moncton approach control and requested an approach to landing. It was granted immediately and we were informed that no other instrument traffic was using the airport. We were cleared for the approach. The navigator had dug out the approach plate for Moncton and gave a copy to each of us. The two pilots were four or five feet apart and it wasn't reasonable to share a copy. The approach was straightforward, simple outbound track, do a procedure turn [a 45 degree turn, fly for a minute, an 180 degree turn back to the track] and intercept the inbound bearing to the station.

Due to the single engine performance we planned the descent to cover the whole approach and not level off. This amounted to reducing one descent to avoid a level off on the inbound track. The weather was getting worse, but still flyable, plus another 'but,' the wind favored the wrong runway for our approach. Normally, the approach would be completed with a straight-in final approach and landing. In this case, we were going to have to land in the opposite direction to the approach, making that 180 degree turn back with the one remaining engine.

Major Emmons started the approach and we kept a running chatter about where we were and what was happening. I told him I would keep the landing gear up until landing was assured. He agreed. He made a good approach, considering the type of radio equipment we were using and the accuracy it represented. We used the ADF [Automatic Direction Finding] needle that pointed to the radio beacon and compared this with the compass to maintain the track over the ground. [in retrospect, I suppose three or four planes could make approaches at the same time and the inherent inaccuracies would prevent a mid-air collision.] The needle pointing to the radio beacon was not a rock steady pointer but wavered as the loop antenna could not measure it precisely. Any heading change by bank or yaw caused the needle to seesaw on the instrument. We made a continuous chatter 'Left five', 'airspeed is OK', 'Right five', 'Right another five,' 'Ease up on the descent.' We were still in the descent passing the station and continued the descent to the minimum altitude. No luck! At minimums, we were in the scud with momentary ground contact. We believed this crate wouldn't climb out for a missed approach, so it was this approach or none.

"Down another 100 feet!" I called out and gave him a corrected heading to the airport. Finally, at about 200 feet above the ground we 'broke out' and just then we saw the airport at our 10 o'clock. 'Damn!' Wrong side of the runway. We would have to turn into the dead engine. I called out 'full power coming up' and moved the right engine prop and throttle levers to full power. Perry corrected with more right trim and held the heading solid. We were too near to the airport to make a turn to get on the other side of the runway. We had to keep the runway in sight all the time. It was going to be a left turn to the runway, no way around it.

Good spacing for the downwind leg, and I checked in with the control tower, "Air Force 575 downwind, emergency landing." They acknowledged. At this point, we found out later, the tower operator saw the C-82 in that nose high attitude and what looked like stall speed, and pushed the CRASH BUTTON, to call out the fire trucks and rescue. It looked bad!!

The C-82 was doing a good job, the airspeed was in a safe range [yes, slow too] but we had to make an 180 degree turn back to the runway. At the proper point, Perry started his turn to base and final approach very carefully and precisely. I reminded him that I would lower the gear at the last second. He agreed again. The old plane came around the turn with nothing to spare and Perry lined up with the runway center line not far from the end of the runway. I knew how many seconds it took to lower the gear. It was electric and was very consistent, each wheel having its own motor to move the landing gear. When it became apparent to do the deed, I moved the landing gear handle to the DOWN position, and called out 'Gear Down !! ' The end of the runway went under the windshield and the three green lights indicating gear down and locked came on. Perry flared the big cargo plane slightly and planted it on the ground. He stopped the plane on the runway easily and we all let out a loud cheer!

In a short while, the ground crew at Moncton airport came out with a tug, the flight engineer got out our tow bar and we were towed to a parking spot. By the end of the day, one of the air base cargo planes came in from Harmon and gave us a lift home. It ended an exciting flight that ended well, with no hits and no errors.

THE REST OF THE STORY. I thought that was the end of the story for a few days anyway and was happy it worked out so well, considering the factors working against us. Perry Emmons and I were put in for the Air Medal, but the powers that be thought the glory belonged to the pilot in command, so he got the Air Medal [which I think was later downgraded as well] and I ended up with a verbal ATTA BOY award and a clap on the back.

A maintenance team was sent back to Moncton to fix the airplane, to include a complete cleaning off of the oil. It turned out the leak was from the same cylinder that had been changed at Westover AF Base. The cylinder had stripped the threads on the mounting bolts and lifted them off the engine case. That repair was assisted by a civilian Moncton machinist. The boss sent me to Moncton to test hop and return the plane to Harmon AF Base. I arrived with a co-pilot, the same flight engineer from the original flight and some parts the mechanic needed to complete the work.

The plan was to make a thorough pre-flight, ground engine run-up, re-check the installation of the cylinder and time permitting, leave for Harmon. I had not known how much fuel was on the plane on the flight before, but something told me it wasn't enough fuel– something to do with the flight from Mobile. So the flight engineer transferred all of the fuel from the inboard tanks to the outboard tanks where the fuel could be checked visually by putting a dipstick in the tank. Lo and behold, we didn't have enough fuel to get to Harmon and didn't the day of the engine failure. It would have been close with both engines running at cruise, but with one engine at full power at a slower speed, there was clearly a shortage of fuel. 'Jesus! What if we had pressed on to Harmon?'

That rattled my bones, but we refueled the plane with plenty of fuel and the mechanics started to perform an engine run-up test to confirm everything was working. They decided to start the right engine as well since it hadn't been run-up for several days. I stood off to one side of the plane with the man acting as the fire guard and watched the engine start. The left engine huffed and puffed and started and was soon running at fast idle. They started the right engine, the stalwart engine that brought us into Moncton safely. It huffed and puffed and roared to life. WOW ! ! OIL ! OIL came pouring out of the bottom of the right engine!. The fire guard was frantically giving the 'cut engine' signal and waving his arms. They quickly shut down the engine followed by the left engine. They quickly got out to join us at the right engine. There was at least five gallons of oil on the ground and still dripping. The mechanics quickly removed the lower part of the engine cowling or metal cover to see what had happened.

In short, the engine oil sump had broken loose from the engine case and oil was being pumped out.. The oil sump's job is to pump oil back into the oil tank since the round or radial engines operate without an oil pan, unlike an automobile that stores oil in the oil pan. When the oil sump separated, the oil was being pumped out under pressure and would empty the oil tank in a few minutes and the engine would quickly seize. -- 'Holy Baloney !' What kept it from popping off in flight?

The cheese got more binding when I found out that the original cylinder change at Westover AF Base was accomplished, one step was omitted. After a new cylinder is installed and the engine is run-up to check the perfomance, the new cylinder nuts are re-torqued to proper specs to prevent the mounting studs from becoming unevenly stressed. The second re-torquing of the cylinder was not done.

So the flight boiled down to a series of errors that should have resulted in a fatal accident, but it didn't happen. Why?

1] If the original cylinder change at Westover had been done properly, the engine would have performed normally and the flight would have continued to Newfoundland, except that the fuel on board was questionable. My estimate back then was the dry tanks would have occurred 10 – 20 miles from Harmon AF Base.

2] The maintenance failure causing the oil leak and the subsequent landing at Moncton might have saved a sudden loss of engine power if the right engine oil sump had failed instead. No one can say whether the oil sump would have separated or if it did, where it would occur.

3] There was no excuse for the low fuel in the airplane since we were not carrying any cargo, and the fuel load was carried to do the job and then some. An issue with one fuel gauge was the cause for confusion. For the life of me, I can't remember why I questioned the fuel load that day at Moncton.

The eventual flight, from Moncton to Harmon after the sump was repaired and double checked, was a normal flight with plenty of fuel and normal – normal operation. It was later in the week when the events came together and we started looking into the details.

I had many other interesting flights in the C-82, including one where we almost ran out of fuel on a flight over the Iceland ice cap – but that is a different story.

FLYING THE C-82 AT KEFLAVIK, ICELAND

The C-82 Packet [above] was a great airplane in its day and served as a general hauler of many things for the Air Rescue Service. It could carry a large variety of cargo, lots of passengers, and large cargo – at least in that time, and was a of the art cargo aircraft. It was assigned to several Air Rescue Squadrons simply to haul another airplane or helicopter.

I read a fancied tale of the C-82 towing two L-13 Liaison planes to the search area. [right] I can't imagine this being done in real life, but considering the expected frequency of engine failures on the L-13, towing it to the search area would put the L-13 where you knew where to search, following the inevitable engine failure.

The C-82 could carry the L-13 inside the cargo compartment after turning the landing gear inward, retracting the wings and elevators. This would be preferable to towing it. The H-5 helicopter could also fit inside the cargo compartment. It was a wonderful way to get the slow, short range helicopter to a distant air base to complete a rescue mission. And that is what we were doing in this mission.

In the late 40s and 50s, there was a need to get large numbers of jet fighters to Europe and the old fashioned way of using a boat was not satisfactory. These were the days before in-flight refueling and jet fighter range was in the neighborhood of 600-700 nautical miles. The plan then was to island hop from the US to Europe, via Labrador, Greenland, and Iceland. It was a dangerous operation: Short range aircraft short of fuel at each stop, unpredictable weather, and long stretches of overwater with little of no navigation aids. These operations carried a code name of FOX ABLE [Fighter Atlantic] along with a number showing the sequence.

Fox Able One was the first such mission, a test to see if it was feasible. These crossings had little in the way of navigation and fuel was critical. Once they arrived at Goose Bay, Labrador, it was basically an overwater flight. The route took them from Goose Air Base to Narsarsuaq [Nar sar sue wak], Greenland, then on to Keflavik, Iceland. They would have an overnight rest. then the flight to Scotland. During the movement of jet fighters, the authorities moved the stationary weather ships to locate them on the jet fighter's track. The weather ships would broadcast a low-frequency radio signal and the automatic direction finders in the jets could come close to the weather ship and get an accurate time over the ship to establish the ground speed. The Air Rescue Service started placing an orbiting amphibian or SB-17 along the track and located between the weather ship and the land on either side. With any luck then, the fighters had three semi-accurate navigation points on each overwater leg.

For this particular Fox Able, the Air Rescue people decided to put a helicopter at Narsarsuaq, Once in place the helicopter would be able to pick up survivors if things didn't work out, or pick the pilots up after they ejected. Narsarsuaq was called Bluie West One in those days, and I was assigned to carry the helicopter there in the C-82. [For simplicity, I will call the air base BW-1, the name it was best known by in 1951 when this took place.] Loading the H-5 helicopter into the cargo compartment was a job, but the mechanics did it without any problems. It was a tight fit even after the various appendages were removed. And it was heavy too, but we still had enough fuel for what we needed. The approach into BW-1 was via a 40-mile long fiord unless the clouds were very high and they could descend at the airport visually

Mid-morning of Sept 12, 1950 we launched for Goose Bay Air Base for fuel before heading for BW-1. As you can imagine, in 1950 the movement of these jets was classified, and a funny thing happened during the stop at Goose. As any other flight, we had been cleared to fly into Goose Bay, but once we got on the ground and parked a jeep came roaring up to the plane. A full Colonel got out any started yelling at me. The same incident covered in the PBY accident story.

The next day, with enough fuel stuffed in the C-82 we departed for BW-1. The flight from Goose Bay to Greenland was uneventful, but always full of questions about navigation and weather. We passed by the weather ship as indicated by our radio compass, but we were on top of the clouds and didn't see the ship. It is somewhere near 700 nautical miles from Goose to BW-1, and other than a radio fix leaving the Labrador coast and the weather ship, the navigation is pretty much dead reckoning, fly the flight plan headings and hope they are right. In those days, it was always a threat and a bit of anxiety due to the constantly changing magnetic variation, unknown winds aloft and changeable weather. On this day, the weather at the airport was OK, but not good enough to descend directly from the local non-direction radio beacon. We proceeded to the radio beacon out at the coast in order to locate the correct fjord leading to the airport at BW-1.

This radio beacon was located at Simiutaq [Simi u tak], Greenland, a non-directional radio located very close to the fjord leading to the airport at BW-1. It was important to make good that landfall since there were other fjords that looked like they were on the correct heading to the airport, but they did not end up at the airport. We descended well west of the radio beacon and luckily got below the clouds. It was still daylight and we followed the radio compass needle until we had a visual on the fjord and we kept checking the maps to ensure it was the correct fjord. The trip up the fjord is about 40 miles to the airport, and while it was easy this day, the weather could go down part way to the airport. We had been briefed to stay close to one side or the other so we could do a quick 180 turn if the weather went sour. Passing the grounded ship that was in this fjord confirmed we had the right fjord. Whew-w-w. We also saw the remains of a crashed A-26 that had been there since the war. Coming around the last bend in the fjord, we stayed close to the left side in order to make an easy right 90 degree turn to the runway. The runway was runway 7, an unusual runway in that the approach end was relatively level for 500 to 800 feet then rose steeply for the remainder of its five or six thousand foot length. As I remember, the runway was 118 ft difference in elevation from one end to the other. Nice ! if you are landing uphill, you stop pretty quickly.

At this point, it is fair to mention that takeoff was almost always downhill. The planes really accelerated quickly coming down the hill and had plenty of speed to fly. We knew that to stop the plane going downhill would be nearly impossible before going into the fjord, but that was the way it was.

We settled down for the evening while the poor ground crew unloaded and set up the H-5 helicopter to be ready in the morning. They reported in later that it was ready to go except for the engine run-up and tracking the blades to ensure they were installed correctly. The weather had other ideas. We were on standby for the next few days.

On the third day, someone in the 'higher headquarters' wanted us to carry some much-needed cargo to Sondestrome [an air base further north]. Sondestrome was known as BW-8 during the war and during the time of this story. A route check pilot was provided, the cargo loaded and off we went. The flight was uneventful as far as incidents go, the weather was excellent up on top, and the scenery was spectacular. Ice cap to the east, rough grassless mountains to the west. The approach into Sondestrome was easy in this great weather and we landed without difficulty. While we were taxiing to the cargo area I could see many people out there waving their hands. I remarked to the check pilot that they must be a friendly bunch of people to be waving like that. He laughed and told us that we would soon find out that they were not waving at us.

No, they weren't waving at us, they were swatting at the huge mosquitoes that are found in the arctic areas. Strange though, I never remember them at Narsarsuaq. Needless to say, after the cargo was unloaded, the doors were all closed and three bug bombs were set off. We happily departed to go back to BW-1 and leave the big mosquitoes behind.

Two days later, on 18th, the F-84s flew over on their way to

Keflavik. The weather cooperated and none of them had to make a landing or the approach up the fjord. At some point, the operations indicated that the F-84s had gone far enough that none would turn around to come back to BW-1. Once the last flight had passed, the helicopter that had been sitting on immediate alert took off for a short training flight and look around the area. After the helicopter landed, the ground crew started dismantling it.. Late in the evening at the club we got the word that Operations at the Rescue headquarters advised that they had a ski-wheel SC-47 down on the big Iceland icecap. Their plan was to use the helicopter to bring the crew out. The ski-wheel SC-47 had been involved in a rescue mission to pick up someone on the ice cap and couldn't reach the necessary speed for the takeoff. Rescue operations ordered us to get the H-5 and crew to Keflavik as soon as possible. We alerted all concerned and headed for our rooms to get some sleep.

The helicopter was in the C-82 when we got down to the flight line in the morning. The engineer loaded the maximum amount of fuel allowed to keep us at/below the maximum takeoff weight of 54,000 pounds. There was a weather delay to clear away a little fog, but after the fog lifted we were left with a reasonably high ceiling. We could see the ridge line to the west of the airport so that would allow us to depart via the non-directional beacon and climb out in the weather towards the west and lower mountains. The plan was to reverse course once high enough to turn back to the beacon and climb out eastbound towards Bluie East 3, a weather station and beacon on the east coast. BE-3 would give us a known position to depart from on the long leg to the weather ship on that side of Greenland and Keflavik beyond. As we expected, we got to make that thrilling downhill takeoff and lifted off early. We entered weather passing the first ridge in the climb out to the west and stayed in the weather. We started to pick up ice immediately on the wings and props. We finally reversed course to climb out eastbound over the icecap, but we could not reach our cleared altitude of 13,000. We kept pumping alcohol to the props, but it didn't seem to be working. The wing anti-icers, using exhaust heat, seemed to work OK. The engineer told us he checked the alcohol quantity for the prop anti-icing and it was OK. It was a struggle, but we finally reached 12,000 feet, which was the westbound minimum altitude, so it should be OK to clear all mountain peaks.

The ice on the props was going to be a long-term problem, because it would reduce the range and greatly increase the danger if an engine failed. The remaining engine couldn't keep us flying. The engineer went down to the prop alcohol tank and looked in again with a flashlight. He told us it was a shock to see lots of 'slivers' of ice stuck in the filter. He used a broom handle to break them up and the flow of alcohol started immediately. Slowly the ice started coming off the props, hitting the fuselage with a welcome 'biff' 'bang', the hammer-like pops seemed like the nails being pulled back out of our coffin. Once we were clear of the ice cap, out over the east coast of Greenland, we descended to a lower altitude where we could be between layers. We landed at Keflavik late in the afternoon. The local Rescue Operations Officer told us to get some sleep because we would be flying early in the morning.

Eating supper at the club, our discussion came around to the area east of BW-1 and the problem of the high mountains. I told about having to cross over at the wrong altitude because of icing. One of the SB-17 pilots told of his trip two days earlier that was clear and unlimited visibility. They came over the top at 11,500 ft. under visual rules and were 'looking up at the peaks.'

While we were en route to Keflavik the planners came up with another idea to get the ski-equipped SC-47 off the ice cap east of Reykjavik, the capitol of Iceland. Instead of using the helicopter to lift out the aircrew, they would drop JATO bottles into the site and the 47 could fly itself out. [JATO is for jet-assisted takeoff – but the units were actually solid rockets] Oh yes, we were the only crew with an aircraft that had a nifty way to air deliver stuff. So we would not unload the helicopter, but fill up with fuel and replace the plane that was flying over the SC-47. So off to bed we went with plans for a very EARLY takeoff.

The wing of the hotel where we stayed on the airport was having a loud party. Nothing bad mind you, but impossible to sleep. I dozed through a lot of the noise and finally at some un-godly hour the operations people came around to wake us up to go fly. While we 'slept' the support group people got all of the supplies rounded up, packaged for air drop and loaded in the C-82. Our crew was adjusted to remove the helicopter pilot and ground crew and augmented with people to handle the equipment during the drop. We briefly discussed the methods for delivery, speed, altitude and intercom language and procedures. It was still dark when we got off the ground, probably 4 am or so. . According to my log book, we flew 3:25 before sunrise, and that should have been around 7:30.

The ice cap where the ski-wheel SC-47 [aka Gooney Bird] was located was on the biggest of the three ice caps on Iceland, and about a hundred sixty nautical miles from Keflavik, so we arrived in about an hour and relieved the aircraft and crew that had been 'capping' them during the night. They gave us a quick briefing on what was going on. In summary, the crew on the Gooney Bird were asleep to get some rest before time to get up. They were sleeping in sleeping bags inside the plane. We set up a lazy orbit around the aircraft on the ice cap and set the engine power for maximum endurance. We droned on in the dark and I was very sleepy. It was more than 24 hours since I got up yesterday at BW-1 and got very little sleep at the hotel. After a while, I asked the co-pilot to fly while I took a nap. He gladly took the plane. We were on autopilot by that time. I slouched down in the seat and went to sleep.. .z z z z

I woke up at some point in the bright sunshine, groggy and confused and asked what was going on. The other pilot told me they had already dropped the packages for the breakfast of the crew on the ground and were waiting for them to call for the remainder of the air drop – especially the JATO bottles. I wondered what time it was and looked at my watch. I couldn't figure out the time. I was so groggy, the time didn't check out. I tried figuring out how long we had been in the air by subtracting the takeoff time from the time on the watch. I couldn't make it compute. I finally put my finger on the face and counted the hours since takeoff – 1 2 3 4 5 6 7. HOLY BALONEY !!! We have stayed here too long! We are a long way from the airport and getting low on gas! My memory now is that we were then at the time I had filed for landing time – or close.

That cleared my head and loudly brought it to the attention of the others. We need to get this stuff out of the plane and head for Keflavik. We called the crew on the ground and told them of the need to continue the air drops. We set up a pattern and airspeed for the drop. I checked with the flight engineer about the fuel state, and he told me what he thought was in the tanks. The outboard tanks were reading low, and they seemed to be the accurate tanks on this airplane. We thought we had quite a bit of fuel left in the inboard tanks since this is where the engineer kept his 'extra' stash of fuel. I called out that I was switching to the inboard tanks to run them dry, then deal with the outboard tanks. We turned final approach for the first drop, descended to drop altitude and the co-pilot called the drop of the first JATO bottle. I started a shallow climbing turn to the downwind leg. Just before roll-out on the downwind leg someone called out the right inboard fuel pressure fluctuating. - - the tank is going dry! Or sucking air for some reason. I 'just knew' that it was a dry tank based on my memory of the other low fuel situation over Moncton, Nova Scotia. We switched that engine back to the outboard tank.

That settled it, we were in more trouble than just landing low on fuel – we might not have enough to get back to Keflavik! I asked the co-pilot to tell the crew on the ground we were going to be using a closed pattern due to low fuel and for them to not retrieve anything until we finished. The remaining drops were from a very short racetrack pattern as we got things out of the plane and put on to the target. After the last item left we turned west towards Keflavik and set up long-range power settings on the engines. We elected to put the right engine back on the inboard tank to make sure we got all of the fuel. About 160 nautical miles to go and not much fuel to get there. The aircraft that was to relieve us was approaching the ice cap and checked in on the radio. We briefed them on the situation and started concentrating on getting the most miles out of that fuel load.

The navigator volunteered: "Jones, I wonder if something happens and we have to bail out, will you be charged with one accident or two – Since we have that helicopter on board?" Encouraging words for sure. A little black humor, but I don't recall anyone laughing.

I pulled the RPM lever back a little more, moved the throttles further forward, and leaned the fuel mixture out of auto lean into manual lean. That is what Lindbergh did in the P-38 and it should work for us. Of course, there was no setting in the operating manual for this high manifold pressure accompanying the low RPM. The flight engineer offered that it would be OK as long as the engine was running smooth. Five minutes went by and I reduced the RPM a little more and moved the throttle up a little. Follow that with a slight nudge back on the mixture control. We went through the control trim settings to ensure the aircraft was flying cleanly with no extra drag. The lower power brought more distance but of course we were going slower. This was not a happy scene. We discussed different alternatives, including jettisoning some things that could be moved. We were already pretty much left with a few life rafts and toolkits. We elected to not jettison anything. We actually were in the position of being low on fuel without knowing how much that was. We were looking out of the windshield for possible landing sites if things really went bad, but the terrain was really rough. It would be better to bail out, figuring the law of averages would mean some men would land without breaking anything.

The navigator pointed out that we were flying into a 10-knot wind that was extending our time en route, and we needed to descend a little to reach a lower headwind. As a compromise, believing that the lower altitude meant lower true airspeed, at about 100 nautical miles from Keflavik, we decided to start a very gentle descent that would end at the air base. Very slow descent, a long way to go, but we could bring the RPM back a little more and move the throttle only a small amount. We would be getting more manifold pressure as we descended. Somewhere in the descent, the fuel finally ran dry in the right inboard tank. The left inboard tank ran dry about five minutes later. Jesus, now we could see on the gauges how little fuel we had! And that made me more nervous because it was a miserable amount!

This was taking a long time, and much discussion about a minimum descent altitude so we would have enough altitude when the tanks went dry. Two thousand feet ought to be enough since we would leave when the first engine quit, not the second engine. Off in the distance, we could see the outline of the shoreline defining the town near the airport and it looked pretty good! Also, closer to us, we could see the town of Reykjavik and there was an airfield there too. It looks about 20 to 25 miles from the Reykjavik airport to the Keflavik airport, and what a shame it would be to have the engines quit in between. The co-pilot looked up the airport information as it became larger in the windshield, and it was an inviting sight. We measure the problems and trouble with landing at the civilian field versus the embarrassing events following a bail-out. Mother Nature had a vise-grip on my heart. Jesus! If even one engine runs out of gas, we are goners! But it is only 20 - 25 miles, how much gas is that! How accurate are those gauges? I was looking for a sign to help me make the right decision. . .

And then the sign came: At 2500 feet and within a steep angle to the airport, that airport looked so inviting I couldn't pass it up. I decided that enough was enough and closed the throttles to idle and set the engine mixture for landing. We contacted the tower and declared minimum fuel and requested permission to land. There was no traffic and the tower quickly gave the 'Clear to Land' call and gave us the longest runway into the wind. Before landing checklist! The 'glide' worked out just fine and little or no extra power above idle was required to reach the final approach and get slowed down for landing. Landing gear – DOWN. Flaps – DOWN. The landing was uneventful and we taxied to the operations to find out how and where to get fuel.

Following the hour or so of worrying about running out of fuel, once we were on the ground, the co-pilot and I got giddy. Do I know how Lindberg felt when he got on the ground at Paris?? You betcha. That was the same feeling of being on the ground there at Reykjavik, out of the jaws of death or embarrassment and into a new beginning! Once out of the aircraft and talking to the ground refueling people, I was concerned about how to pay for the fuel. The man in charge said it was the same company that serviced at Keflavik and the same forms and the same price. I couldn't believe my blind luck! With that giddy feeling of gotten away with something, I told the engineer to fill it to the maximum weight. Can you believe such luck?

An operations man wanted to take us somewhere to get something to eat before we took off. Oh yes, we hadn't eaten, hadn't thought about eating, did not feel any hunger, was not thirsty, but now that you mention it. . . He arranged for the ground people to take the engineer and another airman to get something to eat after the plane was refueled. He took us to a place in town where we each got a nice sandwich.

One of the memories of the trip into town was the lack of smoke coming from some houses. Our 'guide' brought out the story of the old city of Reykjavik that was actually heated by the warm water from the hot springs to the east. None of these houses needed other means of heating their houses; however the houses in the new part of the city could not be supported by the hot springs, so each one had their own heating system, and each one had a column of smoke coming up from the chimney.

We got back to the airport and once everyone was collected, we checked over the aircraft and climbed in to go to Keflavik. We were going through the checklist when the co-pilot said, "We have a problem."

That is all I needed, another problem. "What is the problem?' and he gave me a rundown on the gross weight of the plane, the expected takeoff distance and then pointed out that the runway was slightly shorter than our takeoff distance. What! After all this, I will have to sell some fuel back to these nice people? No, they don't buy back fuel. We gave it some serious thought, the difference in distance was not much, more technical than anything, so we decided to make a VERY short take off on that runway.

The engines checked out perfectly – as R-2800 engines do frequently, and after lining up on the runway to use every useable foot, we set the brakes and ran the engines to maximum power. Once the engineer was satisfied they were putting out everything they had, he told us 'OK.' I released the brakes and the beast rumbled down that runway, but it was accelerating nicely. At the end of the pavement, we raised the nose and the old C-82 lifted off like a butterfly – flying nicely, but a little herky-jerky. Gear UP! As soon as we had the airspeed required, we retracted the flaps used for takeoff and accelerated to climb speed for that cross country flight of 20 – 25 miles to Keflavik.

After getting back in the air and feeling giddy again, the co-pilot and I came to the same thought - we were slightly overweight for landing! Not by much mind you, a technical thing, but pilot error is created by technical things. Well, nothing to do but really, I mean REALLY, grease the thing in on the landing. We did just that and it seemed easier than most times when the airplane was light. Probably an element of paying close attention to things added to the smooth landing.

The rescue operations people were glad to get us back and our explanation of needing to land at Reykjavik was accepted as a routine change of plans. I should mention that if any damage had occurred, or any paint scratched, there would have been many questions that started: "Why the hell did you __________? . . . . . But, the Operations Officer had a request: The plane flying orbit now is on his way back with engine trouble. Can you get back out there until we can round up someone else?

What can you say? With all the luck we've had, nothing can go wrong. So we launched again for what was a three or four hour flight until a replacement crew got up to the site. The total flight time for that day was twelve hours and 45 minutes and four landings. Crew duty day? They hadn't invented that term back in 1950, but it was a reasonable 15 – 16 hours probably.

I should mention that the SC-47 crew were rescued from the icecap by an Icelandic rescue group with dog sleds. This group was on the way while we were attempting the rescue. The JATO bottles were not enough to push the plane through the snow to reach takeoff speed. The SC-47 was removed years later by an Icelandic team. My memory is that the snow conditions at takeoff for the SC-47 were such that the snow did not pack, so the skis plowed through. Sometimes this is called 'corn snow.'

A C-82 with a T-6 Texan trainer in the background [file photo]

After waiting for favorable weather for four days, we departed Keflavik. The mission ended after landing back at Ernest Harmon AF Base, preceded by the usual overwater flights back through BW-1 and Goose Bay with little or no navigation information, but accomplished by fear-of-failure and a whole lot of luck.

FLYING THE SA-16 ALBATROSS IN AIR RESCUE

[from USAF Training Film]

The Grumman Albatross SA-16 was a fun plane to fly, and maybe the toughest plane I ever flew. The construction was made to take the heavy beating of an ocean landing, and after flying the PBY it seemed a step up in strength and luxury. This amphibian had a floor instead of a catwalk, comfortable seats, insulation, and an interior. The plane had other improvements that included the quick feathering prop; and a new method that improved winter operation. The propeller had an oil supply of a very thin oil to provide better and quicker operation. The feathering process was very quick compared to the other propeller/engine combinations in use in those times. The propeller was very loud, and the tip speeds could surge up to near supersonic speeds.

On occasion the quick feathering feature may have saved the propeller and engine nose section from separating from the engine. During a training flight, I was going through engine out procedures with a pilot who was close to qualification in the aircraft. Trying to keep him from knowing which engine I was going to fail, I had my left hand up out of his sight on one of the fuel selectors. Without any lesser warning, the right engine started a sudden and rapid vibration. I decided to push the feathering button near my hand, rather than have the student shut the engine down. The prop stopped immediately, and later we completed the engine shutdown checklist. We made a routine one engine landing back at the home base.

While we were being towed in, the pilot asked the obvious question: "Since we have been practicing the full procedure for an engine failure, why did you just push the feathering button?" Alas, the checklists are a guide and a standard to prevent mistakes, but the vibration was such that I felt stopping the engine was the most important thing to do. As it turned out, a reduction gear in the nose section of that R-1830 had failed, and the nose section had a crack nearly ¼ of the circumference. I believe that had I decided to tell him to shut it down, the prop and nose section would have separated from the engine, and the prop could have come in the cockpit.

Later while stationed with Headquarters Air Rescue Service, I was assigned to the standardization board for the SA-16. This job gave me lots of travel over the world to give check rides and find interesting places to fly. Most of the flights were routine, but the worse flight was during a search mission. I was in England to give some check rides to the Rescue unit stationed there. The day before I arrived, a B-36 ditched in the North Atlantic west of Ireland and they were organizing the search. I volunteered to fly in the right seat and observe the pilot and help as needed. The weather was lousy in the search area, and aircraft from all over the UK were responding. They assigned search areas around a weather ship that moved into the main area for the purpose of providing aid and a radio beacon for the search aircraft.

We arrived early into the area and descended to VFR under the low clouds. The ceiling was less than 500 ft. and we put out the Pilot Report of the weather to all. One by one, the aircraft arriving on-scene contacted us and asked for information and instructions. We elected to set up an ad hoc Air Traffic Control function right there in the cockpit. Using a map provided by the navigator and a notebook, we started issuing permissions for the descent into the area, while not allowing two aircraft in areas next to each other. Exact navigation was difficult, and high winds and low ceilings made for a dangerous search.

The wind over the water was close to 45 knots, and the seas were higher than I ever experienced. A water landing for our amphibian would have been fatal. We didn't see anything in our search area, but we heard B-

29s had dropped boats to survivors, so we knew there was some success. As it turned out there were four survivors located and saved, three saved by one boat parachuted to them and one man receiving the other dropped boat. Ships picked up the survivors.

Years later, trying to verify some of the facts and refresh my memory, I could not locate any information about a B-36 that ditched in the Atlantic off the Irish coast. My flight record didn't give any details that helped either. About the time I had doubts about remembering the incident, I discussed the subject with a daughter. She quickly found two newspaper articles from Ireland that gave news details confirming the Aug 5, 1953, ditching, and subsequent rescue. Memory refreshed.

FLYING THE T-39

Assignments after flying the SA-16 took me into more modern aircraft and equipment technology. Leaving Air Rescue Service led me to the T-33 in preparation for an assignment as a Tac Recon Pilot flying the RB-57A and the RB-66 with the 1st Tactical Recon Squadron in Spangdhalem, Germany. The RB-57 was a good two engine jet, easy to fly – reminded me of the B-25 - and could go to 50.000 feet without a struggle. The two engines were probably a little too far from the centerline, which made it touchy on one engine. Loss of an engine before the Safe Single Engine Speed of 166 knots could be dicey.

The RB-66 development delayed getting the aircraft to the tactical units, so we flew them as brand new aircraft with the little curly aluminum pieces from the drill bits here and there. Good navigation radar, good cruise and 'Get out of Dodge Speed', and could continue climb out on one engine after retracting flaps during takeoff. It produced 10,000 pounds of thrust, but it took several seconds to reach the exhaust gas temperature needed to ensure the full thrust. Despite this, it could make a go-around from short final. One feature of the RB-66 was the ability, according to the Pilots Handbook, to be able to fly above the speed of sound under certain circumstances. I was asked one time to fly as fast as it would go and have the gunner rotate the 20mm gun turret. The idea was to check an improvement they were testing. I tried, diving from 35,000 ft. to 16,000 at full throttle without exceeding .98 Mach. The irony of flying a plane that was allowed to exceed the speed of sound, but wasn't able to do it was not lost on us. Later in that tour, I was transferred to 12th AF Hqs. as a Recon Staff Officer, flying the T-33 for proficiency and the RB-66 to stay in touch.

Following the tour in Germany, I was disappointed to be assigned to an RC-121D unit, the 551st Airborne Early Warning Wing. The RC-

121D also required the services of a recon pilot. The RC-121D is a good airplane, but the flying requires too many people on board. Sometimes 26 people were onboard, each with a specific job. The preflight briefing looked more like a staff meeting. The plane was safe and did its job very well.

I escaped the RC-121D for a tour in 5th Air Force Hqs. in Japan, using my recon pilot job description [called the AFSC – AF Specialty Code] as the crutch. As a result, I had the opportunity to fly the North American T-39 for proficiency. The T-39s were busy flying all over, and I enjoyed that.

Most flights were carrying people or parts around the region. Some preplanned and some on short notice. One such trip was to fly from Yokota Air Base to Thailand to deliver a Wing Commander and one fighter pilot to an air base there. The flight was planned through Okinawa to the Philippines to DaNang, Vietnam, and then to Taklhi Air Base, Thailand. After delivery of the goods, I was to return to Japan. The flight to Okinawa for fuel was routine, but still had to be careful with the navigation. The next leg to Clark Air Base, Philippines had a problem, all the usual altitudes were taken by bombers and tanker planes out of Guam on their way to Vietnam, and Air Traffic Control offered either 44,000 or 14,000 feet altitude. The latter would be too low, because we would use a lot of fuel at that low altitude and wouldn't have enough range to reach the Philippines. 44,000 is above the maximum altitude according to the operating manual, but I had flown the plane nearly that high and selected that and they processed the flight plan. As it worked out, the T-39 [a six place passenger jet] climbed to 44,000 [Flight level 440 as it is called] and flew beautifully, using very little fuel. The cabin altitude was well within the normal level, and we arrived in Clark Air Base without incident or seeing any B-52s or KC-135 tankers.

When I parked on the ramp waiting for the refueling truck, a staff car drove up, and a full colonel got out. Without explanation, he said: " You are going to Tan Son Nhut [at Saigon] right away." and I replied, "No, I am going to Da Nang for fuel and then to Thailand." He reminded me that 'I didn't understand, they are calling in all the T-39s in the area.' A C-135 with a bunch of Generals is at Clark Air Base, and the airplane is grounded. They had to get those VIPs to Tan Son Nhut for a meeting. So the Wing Commander and the Captain fighter pilot took their stuff off the plane, and I promised to come back for them.

Three Generals and a Colonel showed up a few minutes later, and we started up for the trip to Saigon. I had been there before so no problem, but I didn't have time to do the detailed flight planning, and let my copilot do it. I did pick a course to the left slightly; that passed a TACAN site [navigation radio] to give me a more accurate path over the water. This is called a dog leg, and it offered me better navigation but slightly longer flight. I did not get involved with the other three or four T-39s that were involved since I was the first to arrive and depart Clark Air Base. About half way to Saigon, one of the Brigadiers came up to the cockpit and shot the breeze for awhile, and he asked what time we would get to Tan Son Nhut. I didn't know precisely, but quickly making some rough mathematics; I told him '12 o'clock.' But one fellow was behind me close enough to affect my flight. When I got ready for the descent into Tan Son Nhut the traffic control informed me that they couldn't let me descend because of traffic behind me. Our 'safe zones' over the water overlapped. Once we got into radar contact with the traffic people, they gave me the lower altitude fairly close the Tan Son Nhut Normally, in this airplane, we didn't use the speed brakes to slow the plane [considered bad planning] but I had no choice and called out loud over my shoulder "SPEED BRAKES – **NOW** !" The loud roar of the speed brakes confirmed they opened and sounded like the bottom skin is being ripped off the fuselage.

Fortunately, the General that asked for the estimate to landing knew about the delay in descent and could explain to the others. We came down quickly and fast, with the radar people lining us up with the runway very nicely. Gradually slowing the plane to the normal speeds for landing we arrived 'just right' for a nice landing. As I turned off the runway, the clock said 12 noon! Wow ! I couldn't believe it, after guessing at the time. In the business, we would call that 'pulling the number out of the [you know what].' Well, there we were at Tan Son Nhut and my real passengers were at Clark. I quickly refueled, filed the flight plan and went back to Clark. They were waiting patiently (?) and we proceeded back on the original plan to take them to Thailand.

I loved that T-39, but only flew it for the two years I was in Japan. It was the first airplane that I flew that I could lose an engine on the takeoff roll and depending on the air speed; we could stop on the runway or continue the takeoff. This feature is required for transport planes, but other planes don't have the excess power needed. I left the T-39 when I volunteered for Vietnam and the F-100 and never had the chance to fly it again.

Before the Japan tour was up, I had many trips to Vietnam and Thailand, one a one-month temporary assignment to the new Direct Air Support Center (DASC) at Nha Trang, Vietnam as a Recon Staff Officer to fill in until the Personnel people filled the DASC with permanent people.

My Japan tour was cut short when I volunteered to fill one slot in a request to assign two officers to 7th Air Force Hq at Tan Son Nhut. That required a return to the US to check out in the F-100. Arrival at 7th AF revealed they did not have a slot for a Lt Col for me, and they sent me to the 37th Tac Fighter Wing at Phu Cat which was a great place. As a staff officer, I flew almost every day after the local check out.

After flying routine combat missions for six months, I volunteered to become a "Misty FAC," and served as the third Misty commander. Part of a then-classified mission code named "Operation Commando Sabre", whose mission was to choke off the flow of supply trucks along the Ho Chi Minh trail from North Vietnam and prevent SAM deployment in the area of operation. The Mistys flew the F-100 as high-speed forward air controllers to coordinate the effort. The mission was dangerous, and losses were high. All pilots were volunteers. I was Misty 35. That was the most exciting assignment I ever had. Wonderful job, mission, and people. I covered some of those adventures in another book "MISTY First Person Stories of the F-100 Misty Fast FACs in the Vietnam War."

Flying after my return to the States put me back into the RC-121D again, plus flying the C-47, the first time since 1949. The RC-121 Wing moved to California, and I transferred to an EB-57B unit that flew as targets in Air Defense training and exercises. It was an interesting mission with lots of good flights. That squadron was de-activated, and I moved to Burlington, VT along with half of the EB-57s. At Burlington, I was the Senior Advisor to the Vermont Air National Guard and served in that job until retirement.

Finally, I retired from the United States Air Force. I never thought I would make it, but there I was. But my life flying airplanes was not over. After retirement, I flew about 6000 hours in light planes as an instructor pilot, Civil Air Patrol pilot, and charter pilot. Civilian airplanes I flew included: various models of the Piper Cub, and other Piper single and twin engine planes; Cessna-made airplanes including the 152, 172, 182, 210, 310, 340, 402, and Caravan; and Beech-made planes including the Musketeer, Bonanza and two versions of the Baron. I was an instructor in most of these and check airman in those used in the charter business.

A FINAL THOUGHT

During my flying career beginning with my first solo in 1946 and ending with my last flight in 2012, I flew 65 different models of aircraft and 16,000 hours, over period of sixty six years. That means that I spent nearly two thirds of my life pursuing my childhood dream of being a pilot. Looking back on that life, I can honestly say that I was never bored or tired of flying and in fact, enjoyed every minute if it. Would I do it over again? In a heartbeat!

Some readers may find the title of this book misleading because it implies that learning only occurs while one is relatively inexperienced. On the contrary, you continue to add new experiences because flying is an ever-changing environment that offers up new and unexpected challenges. The idea is to learn from yours and other experiences and avoid that terminal challenge that ends the career. With that thought in mind, if just one lesson I described manages to prevent the death or serious accident of a pilot flying today, or even someone in the next generation of pilots, writing this book will have been well worth the effort.

I was always afraid of dying. Always. It was my fear that made me learn everything I could about my airplane and my emergency equipment, and kept me flying respectful of my machine and always alert in the cockpit.

Chuck Yeager

Made in the USA
Columbia, SC
03 September 2024

41540352R00070